Advance Praise for
Be There!

"John has done it again! He has put forth in plain language how to live out one of the most important qualities of healthy human relationships. More clearly than any book we can remember, *Be There!* has shown us how to relate to one another with God's ever-present love. Engaging. Practical. Biblical. Read this book and you will enjoy the blessing of connections that you never dreamed were possible."

—DRS. LES AND LESLIE PARROTT
Seattle Pacific University authors of *Relationships*

"*Be There!* encourages all of us to show up and be 'God with skin on' in the relationships that matter most: those with our spouse, kids, family, and friends. Readers who grew up in be-there homes will smile and tear up all the way through John's heartwarming, encouraging book. Those who didn't will be coached with grace on how to connect to those they love!"

—DR. GARY ROSBERG
president of America's Family Coaches, radio show
co-host, and coauthor (with wife, Barbara) of
The Five Love Needs of Men and Women

"In the business world, 'being there' for a customer or supplier is crucial to being successful. With our families and with our faith, 'being there' is even more important. The message of this book is one John lived out when he worked for me in his seminary days and lives out today in his ministry and family. We believe in John, his ministry, and the message of this book—that we're to be there for others, just the way Jesus has been there for us."

—NORM MILLER
chairman, Interstate Batteries

"Finally—something we can all actually do: *Be There!* John Trent moves us to tackle the daily distractions and make an eternal difference in the lives of our children."

—ELISA MORGAN
president and CEO, MOPS International

"If you want to be a better husband, father, or friend, *Be There!* will help you get there! Packed with fascinating anecdotes, biblical principles, and practical wisdom, Trent's book spells out how we can all have deep, rich relationships—and, after all, isn't that what it's all about?"

—BILL MCCARTNEY
founder and president, Promise Keepers

FOCUS ON THE FAMILY®

BeThere!

Making Deep, Lasting
Connections in a
Disconnected World

John Trent, *Ph.D.*

WATERBROOK
PRESS

BE THERE!

PUBLISHED BY WATERBROOK PRESS

5446 North Academy Boulevard, Suite 200

Colorado Springs, Colorado 80918

A division of Random House, Inc.

With stories retold from *Faith of My Fathers* by John McCain (New York: Random House, 1999); *Courage Is Contagious* by John Kasich (New York: Doubleday, 1998).

ISBN 1-57856-178-7

Published in association with the literary agency of Alive Communications, Inc., 7680 Goddard Street, Suite 200, Colorado Springs, CO 80920

Printed in the United States of America

2000—First Edition

10 9 8 7 6 5 4 3 2 1

To my wife, Cindy,
for "being there" for me these twenty years.
Your name is full of honor and integrity,
your eyes are always looking to support Kari, Laura, and me,
and your heart for the Lord has never once wavered.
I couldn't think of a better person to love forever.

Contents

Contents

1 | *Secret Strength for Sun-Parlor Days*

She should have been bitter and broken and frozen inside.

She had every reason to be.

Every "right" to be, if you want to be politically correct.

Her father had chosen to spend her childhood years far away from his family as he tried and failed to keep a dying farm from sinking into the dust bowl.

Years later, after only a year of marriage, her husband walked into the big sun parlor in their house in Indiana and announced that their relationship was over. There was another woman.

Then came a move to Phoenix to see the sun again. A new start—and one day a new marriage, then the long-awaited birth of children. Three boys—an older son plus a set of twins—in just three years.

Then a replay of the conversation in the Indiana sun parlor: Another husband came home to say there was another woman and he was leaving. No, there would be no further discussion—and in the future, no financial help nor even a card or visit with the boys as they grew up.

The three most significant men in my mother's life all walked away from her: her father when she was a child and then two husbands, who didn't merely leave, but who underscored their sudden departures by choosing someone else over her.

I find it interesting that God gave my mom three young boys to raise. Did the Lord intend this as a way to make up for the missing men in her life? I'm not sure. But I do know that she could have grown full of anger and hurt and shame and self-pity; instead she remained vibrant and alive, warm and loving.

Which always amazed me.

It doesn't usually happen that way.

"We live life as if it were a motion picture," says author Gerald Sittser. "Loss turns life into a snapshot. The movement stops; everything freezes." That's what I've seen over the years in the lives of so many people I've counseled, people who have suffered great loss, people shrink-wrapped and shelved by crushing failures or turned to stone inside because of grief or a love lost forever.

It should have happened to her.

She should have shut down, closed the book on growth and creativity and connection. If not for the people losses she suffered, then certainly for all the physical losses that added injury to insult. Rheumatoid arthritis would twist her hands, tear up her knees, and take away an outstanding career—a corporate vice presidency significant enough to merit a write-up in the *Wall Street Journal.* All ripped away. So too was any realistic chance of remarrying. As her bones dried up, her spirit, too, should have dried and cracked and broken. She should have given up.

Particularly on me.

I was the one who was asked to leave grade school for a stupid mistake. I was the one who police carted home late one night. I was the one who brought home report cards so dismal they wouldn't qualify me to ask, "Paper or plastic?"

But Mom never gave up on life or learning or friends or needy people or the Lord…or her sons. Without a doubt she was the most giving, loving person I've ever known. Even in her last days, she *glowed* (a description given by one of her hospice nurses).

But why?

What enabled her to carry on? What gave her the strength to continue? How could she do it?

After a night of crying out in pain from the arthritis each time she rolled over in bed, she could still greet us with a genuine smile in the morning. For years I wondered how. And what was it that allowed her to look beyond her own pain and loss and "adopt" hurting kids the way other people bring home stray cats? What was it that kept her mind alert and her arthritic fingers still tapping across her computer keyboard? (She got on the Internet before I did!) Why didn't she daily rev up her regrets and hurts, put down my father in front of us, or take the counsel of Job's wife and "turn and curse God"?

What was her secret?

The Brave Choice

Today I realize that she really *did* have a secret—a secret that all of us can discover and learn and use.

Mom had a way of continually connecting to a source of strength and energy and life and recovery and wellness that filled her life to overflowing. In the process she changed so many lives that at her funeral the chapel couldn't begin to contain the throngs who arrived to pay their respects, and those who couldn't get inside hung around outside for the whole service.

What I first saw in my mother, I've since seen reflected in the lives of many courageous, authentic, empowering people of every race, age, and tax bracket. This secret helped Mom keep a positive perspective through all her years of chronic pain and soured relationships.

So what was her secret? What enabled her to thrive—to "glow"—despite the tragedies in her life?

In two words, she chose to *be there* for others. She lifted her eyes to others carrying even deeper hurts.

The template we're given in the Scriptures for how to *be there* is exactly what my Mom followed to connect so deeply with us boys, and it's reflected in countless studies of strong families, great marriages, and deep friendships.

To some, these two amazingly powerful, biblically grounded words—*Be there!*—may sound like a command. My answer is that some of us *need* to hear such a command. For others, these two little words may awaken negative memories of a time when someone important chose not to be there when we really needed them (or even of a time when *we* failed to be there for a loved one).

But for everyone who reads this book, I pray these two simple words will provide a way of escape from past hurts and lukewarm relationships. I hope and expect that, if we listen, they will teach us how to connect at a deeper, more fulfilling level than ever before with our Lord, our loved ones, and people in need.

———

PART ONE

The Benefits of Being There

Let's begin with an up-close and personal look at the very personal benefits that come when we choose to truly, biblically *be there* for others.

Being there is about going beyond casual acquaintances to make deep, lasting connections. To be there for someone adds a sense of mission and purpose to our lives, even as it subtracts fear and isolation. It helps us focus our days and maintain wonder as we age.

Being there for others is reparative therapy for our own broken hearts. Like a subway warden, learning to truly be there will push us through the doors marked *Truth* and *Reality* and wave us away from runaway trains that lead only to denial, pretense, and empty image management.

If you're thinking that these benefits seem to scatter all across the map of our lives, you're right. Like map pins marking every major city and mountain peak across the earth, the benefits of being there stick out in every hemisphere of our lives. I suspect that's because, when we choose to truly be there for others, we live out God's love on earth…and we wind up getting so much in return.

Just like the folks you're about to meet.

2 | *Moms, Dads, and Being There*

George Toles is a close friend who lives in the Seattle area. His day job is running one of the best and busiest independent advertising agencies in that part of the country. His real passion, however, is sharing God's love with business leaders all across the city as well as with his family and friends. We started our friendship by swapping letters, and now e-mail notes fly back and forth almost daily.

George and I have much in common. Both of our dads bailed out when we were young. Both of us came to Christ as young men. Both of us had moms who became the compensating grace of our lives.

In a discussion about our moms, I once told George tongue-in-cheek that my mother was so caring and committed, she could have been a cover girl for *Single-Parent Family* magazine (if such a publication had existed way back then). We each got a laugh out of that. But one day my off-the-cuff statement would come true.

I always thought it was my mother's hands that made her cover-girl material, not that the world would have agreed. My mom's arthritic hands were bent and twisted. Yet I saw how those hands guided, protected, comforted, and in so many ways shaped the lives of three young boys. The arthritis forced her to have only a gentle hold on plates and pens and dishrags…as well as on her sons, whom she loved so much.

That mental picture became the subject of a Mother's Day article I wrote (evolving later into a book) titled "My Mother's Hands." A bonus came when the article was published in Focus on the Family's *Single-Parent Family* magazine—along with a full-page picture of my mom! At last, what I'd known all along became official to everyone else.

Mom was a cover girl!

It was two years too late for Mom to get to see it, but what a wonderful tribute to her nonetheless.

Meanwhile in Seattle, George happened to read the article, saw my mom's photo, and sent me the e-mail message below. For George, it wasn't his mother's hands that made her cover-girl material—it was a scar.

Hi, John,

Yesterday, Mother's Day, was ideal timing for me to read "My Mother's Hands" in *Single-Parent Family*. What a tender, touching tribute to your beautiful mom, Zoa. She was and is a strikingly attractive woman, and I can see you in her eyes. I identified with you so much as I read it. Yet it reminded me of my mother's face, not her hands.

My mother always had a terrible scar on her left cheek. It was the residue of a car accident on the Harrihan Bridge, which crosses the Mississippi River at Memphis. My father was driving and I was an infant in her lap.

A drunk crossed the line and hit us head-on, throwing my mom through the windshield. Praise the Lord, I was only drenched in blood, not injured. Everyone lived, but my mother carried a long scar on her cheek the rest of her life. All of her life, I blessed that scar, knowing that she'd been clinging to me at the moment of impact—just as she clung to me for the rest of her life.

What an incredible picture for George of what it means to *be there*— a sure embrace of her precious child no matter what, leaving a scar that said to George every time he looked at his mother, "I love you, Son. As God gives me strength, I'll always be there for you."

Of course, it's not only mothers who hold on to their kids "no matter what." I've spoken to more than 350,000 men at Promise Keepers conferences across the country. To be sure, not every man returns home as a faithful be-there dad. But many do. And even if some of those fathers are a few years or few pounds beyond their best fighting condition (or even a few hairs short on top), they also rate cover-guy treatment. Why? Because they're men committed to being there for their children. And their kids reap the benefits, as one particular woman with a famous be-there daddy can testify.

A Letter of Love

In 1998 the state of Arizona, the Republican Party, and, in the end, an understanding nation, said good-bye to Barry Goldwater, a man famous for his bold conservatism, his dramatic acceptance speech for the 1964 presidential nomination, and the bolo ties he wore on the Senate floor.

But the senator's fiery speeches and tough exterior aren't what his children took away from their years of growing up under his roof. His eldest daughter, Joanne, gives us a wonderful look at the soft side of her father, a side that proved he was a father who knew how to be there for his children—a side rarely seen by the public.

The following paragraphs are from a priceless letter that Goldwater wrote to twelve-year-old Joanne on June 11, 1948.

Dearest Joanne,

Those beautiful quaking aspens that you've seen in the forest as we have driven along have one purpose in life. I would like to tell you about them because they remind me a lot of Mommy and you kids and me.

Those aspens are born and grow just to protect the spruce tree when it's born. As the spruce tree grows bigger and bigger, the aspens gradually grow old and tired and they even die after a while. But the spruce, which has had its tender self protected in its childhood, grows into one of the forest's most wonderful trees.

Now think about Mommy and me as aspens standing there quaking ourselves in the winds that blow, catching the cold snows of life, bearing the hot rays of the sun, all to protect you from those things until you are strong enough and wise enough to do them yourself. We aren't quaking from fear, but from the joy of being able to see your lives develop and grow into tall, straight men and women.

Just like the spruce, you have almost reached the point where you don't need us as much as you used to. Now you stand like the young spruce, a pretty, straight young thing whose head is beginning to peep above the protection of Mommy and Daddy's watchfulness....

I am telling you all this because from now on a lot of what you eventually become—a lovely woman, a happy woman and a brilliant, popular woman—depends on you.

You can't go through life being these things and at the same time frowning. You can't achieve these things and be grumpy. You have to grow so that your every deed and look reflect the glory that is now in your heart and soul.

Smile. Think right. Believe in God and his worldwide forest of men and women. It's up to you.

I love you,
Daddy

"I still cry every time I read it," Joanne said of this letter in a newspaper article about her memories of her father. "He was a master with words. He was a romantic."

This same political figure who was demonized by liberals in the 1960s as a heartless, cruel warmonger, is seen by his daughter as a loving romantic! That's what can happen when we choose to be there for our children. In a world that will give them more doses of rejection than acceptance, we can provide them with a solid, loving foundation for success that will endure throughout their lifetimes. By being there for our kids, by tenderly expressing our love and warmth and counsel and direction and correction, we enable them to thrive even in difficult circumstances that cause others to take a dive.

And, perhaps sweetest of all—when we determine to be there for our children (as well as for others), the moment arrives one day when we discover they love to be there for us.

The Sweetest Rest

If you've seen the movie *Father of the Bride,* just hearing the title probably brings a smile as you recall watching the nonstop expenditure of energy, time, money, emotion, and laughter that goes into a beloved daughter's wedding. After months of exhausting preparations and hilarious misadventures, a beautiful and surprisingly uneventful wedding takes place. Then, after the reception, Steve Martin (or Spencer Tracy, if you remember the older, black-and-white *Father of the Bride*), slumps into the same easy chair where the movie began.

The disheveled father sits surrounded by scattered rice, dangling streamers, and empty glasses, and reflects on how wonderful the day had been. But the room is also cluttered with memories of how his "little girl" is now all grown up and how much life can change in a single day.

With all the guests finally on their way home, he has certainly earned the right to relax—but he just can't. Something tugs at his elbow like a teenager who wants to go to the mall *now*. It's a nagging insecurity that finally leans over and whispers (in his daughter's voice), "I've got a husband now... Things have changed... I don't need my old dad anymore."

Utter sadness...and then the phone rings.

It's his daughter.

She's calling from the airport, just moments before she speeds away on her honeymoon. The wedding has changed many things in her world, but the most important thing between father and daughter never would, never *could* change. She would always love him—and in the best of ways, she would always be his little girl.

Her call couldn't have been timed any better. There's often a natural low after the highs of any great event. The warmth in her voice and her words of thanks for the wonderful wedding bring a broad smile to his face. It means a great deal to receive a thank-you after all the hard work that goes into putting together a storybook wedding.

But it's her words, "I'll *always* love you, Daddy," that bring a tear of joy to her father—and many more to the audience. That unexpected affirmation of love from the new bride to her father yields an immediate effect. For the first time since the movie began, the father of the bride is able to lean back in his chair and enjoy a much-needed sense of rest.

In the midst of being there for our kids, *rest* is often the last thing we get (if we manage to nab any at all). But Steve Martin and the makers of *Father of the Bride* remind us that the sweetest rest comes not at the beginning of the story, not in the middle, but closer to the end—after the rice has been thrown and the guests have gone home, when your daughter calls from the airport just to say, "I'll *always* love you, Daddy."

If that's not a benefit worth working and waiting for, I don't know what is.

3 | *A Husband Who Won by Being There*

I never got to know my father any deeper than the quarter-inch or so he was willing to share with me. But I got to go in the "deep end" with a wonderful father figure whom God gave to me.

I met Uncle Max while attending college at Texas Christian University. One day I was visiting a neighboring school, Southern Methodist University in Dallas, Texas, when I saw a sign above a door: *Head Librarian—Robert M. Trent.*

As a joke, I walked right into the office and announced that I was Robert M. Trent's long-lost nephew…and nearly fell down when we discovered that I really *was*. I knew few names on my father's side of the family, but there he stood, Robert M. Trent, my *father's* uncle (and my great-uncle), as he explained that he preferred to go by the name Max.

Uncle Max kindly invited me to his home, where I first met his wife, Sarah. They were both Columbia University honors graduates in library science. He became the head librarian at SMU, and she served as an assistant head librarian at the Dallas Public Library. But it wasn't the books spilled all over the house that drew my attention. It was the obvious way that, after forty years of marriage, those two lovebirds still enjoyed a storybook marriage.

Uncle Max opened the door for his bride without fail, and her arm wasn't even broken! When I was there, he first asked *her* what she'd like to drink or snack on, and only then did he ask his guest. You could tell he was smitten with her just from the way he looked at her. And she was equally devoted to him. God hadn't chosen to give them children, but they made up for it in their love for each other.

I grew to love Uncle Max and Aunt Sarah. I felt accepted and even "adopted" by them both. But one day, ten years after meeting them, I noticed that Sarah began to falter with—of all things for a librarian—her words. Names began to slip. Soon that…that…*thing* she was looking for wouldn't quite snap to mind.

A battery of tests eventually determined that Aunt Sarah was suffering from early-onset Alzheimer's disease. The fearsome illness would soon reduce a Columbia honors student to someone in a nursing home, forced to wear a bib, unaware of all she'd lost.

What Husbands and Wives Want Most

But there was one thing Aunt Sarah would never lose—something that experts call the "best" part of a marriage.

Howard Markman is one of our country's leading researchers in identifying the characteristics of strong marriages. In *Fighting for Your Marriage,* a helpful book he coauthored with Scott Stanley and Susan Blumberg, he notes what might be a surprising discovery.

Do you know—*bottom line*—what a husband wants most from a wife and a wife from her husband? No, not sex or a credit card with an unlimited balance. Based on tens of thousands of interviews with husbands and wives, these experts determined that what we seek most in a marriage partner is…

…a *friend.*

Can you imagine?

Out of all the possible choices, a *friend!*

I can imagine it, and I think you can as well. What all of us most desire is a companion to go through time with us, to listen to us, accept us, believe in us.

That's exactly what Uncle Max and Aunt Sarah had in each other. That's what most couples who choose to *be there* for each other have by the time they reach the end of their ride. They know firsthand what Solomon meant when he said of his bride, "This is my beloved and this is my friend" (Song of Solomon 5:16).

But of course, that doesn't mean a ride without bumps.

At the end of Uncle Max and Aunt Sarah's life together, they lost the ability to be friends in the same way they had enjoyed for fifty years of marriage. (And that's not counting the eight years they dated *before* they were married!)

But there would never be an end to Uncle Max's saying, "This is my beloved."

I marveled as I watched him lovingly wrap a sweater around her fragile, stooped shoulders or wipe her mouth after a meal. I watched in awe as I observed him sit and read to her from one of her favorite books. And I gloried as I witnessed him kiss her good-night on the forehead, even though she stared ahead as if she didn't feel a thing or hear a word.

Real Life

In those final years Uncle Max spent with Aunt Sarah, I saw in an inspiring, tearful way what it means to be there for a dearly loved spouse.

I saw that love, rather than being some sentimental trifle, tenderly whispers its poems of devotion through iron teeth.

I saw that being there not only blesses a failing wife but also ennobles a faithful husband.

From someone's choice to be there for an ailing spouse, I saw the benefits spread out like the roots of a tree, bringing life and color and joy to those privileged enough to witness it.

I'm so sorry that in this fallen world Uncle Max and Aunt Sarah had to encounter this illness. But I'm overpoweringly thankful for all they went through as well. I'll always be grateful that even though I grew up in a single-parent home, I got to see, up-close and personal, what real commitment can be like between a husband and a wife.

My Uncle Max didn't have to be there for Aunt Sarah. He could have shuttled her off to the nursing home and returned to "real life" with his own activities and friends. He could have visited her on weekends and holidays, and pursued his own interests the rest of the time, determined to make the most of his twilight years.

But that was not real life for Uncle Max. Had he refused to be there for his darling wife, both she and he would have ended up the big losers.

He's no loser, though, my Uncle Max! When I think of winners, he's right there at the top of my list. Some people might think it cost him to be there for his wife, but if he were still around today, he'd tell you that's absolute rubbish. Uncle Max won big when he married his beloved Sarah, and he won bigger by staying with her to the end.

In a marriage, being there is the path to the winner's circle.

4 | *The Life-Sustaining Power of Be-There Friends*

To read Senator John McCain's inspiring *Faith of My Fathers* gives a clear glimpse of two things. First, the book provides a frightening picture of seven horrific years in a North Vietnamese prison camp. Second, it offers an inspiring picture of how being there as a committed friend can keep others around you sane, strong, and alive.

Although few of us will ever have to forge our friendships in such a terrifying place, the relationships built in those ghastly prisoner-of-war camps can say much to us about what it means to *be there* for a friend. Surviving such mental and physical tortures required having a band of brothers to be there for you.

And who's to say that even in our suburbs and cities and small towns we won't be called upon to survive a war zone of trials and tests? We all need be-there friends—the kind of friends a wounded pilot would count on to survive.

Pledge of Faithfulness

John McCain's ordeal began on a bombing run over Hanoi in early 1967.[1] Just as the lieutenant pulled up the nose of his Navy A-4 fighter-bomber after releasing his bombload, a surface-to-air missile blew off his right wing. McCain remembers pulling the ejection cable but not much else of those first few moments after the explosion. Witnesses said his chute had barely opened before he smashed into a body of shallow water.

He'd landed in the middle of Truc Bach Lake.

In the middle of the city of Hanoi.

In the middle of the day.

There would be no heroic escape. McCain was dragged out of the lake, his body screaming from the pain of a shattered right leg and a broken right shoulder (broken after the first soldier to reach him smashed his rifle butt into it). Denied medical attention, he was taken to a holding cell where he nearly died. But his treatment immediately changed when his captors discovered McCain's father was an admiral in the U.S. Navy. Armed with that news, they rushed him to a hospital.

In time McCain recovered enough from his wounds to join other downed flyers in a prison they called the Plantation. For a year he struggled to recuperate fully from his wounds, all the while enduring terrible conditions, constant harassment, and frequent beatings. Then, one muggy night in June 1968, his dreams for repatriation seemed about to come true.

McCain was summoned to appear before an English-speaking officer whom the prisoners referred to as the Cat. This man was a sadistic, accomplished torturer who enjoyed his work.

McCain went as he was led, still limping badly from his broken leg. By now he was severely underweight and suffering from dysentery.

After nearly two hours of grilling McCain, the Cat suddenly stopped and asked, "Do you want to go home?"

When McCain realized he was hearing a legitimate offer of freedom, the prospect of returning home lifted his withered emotions like an activated ejection seat. He would make it out alive, see his wife, get the medical treatment he needed so badly, sleep on clean sheets, eat warm food! The idea was like every Christmas wish rolled into one.

He was given three days to think over the offer.

Trying to hide his elation, McCain was taken back to his cell. Once there, through a secret communication line, he raised a fellow officer, Bob Craner, to ask his advice. Prisoners caught talking to each other would receive a severe beating, but both men risked it to discuss this incredible offer.

As they talked, McCain began to be troubled by the unwritten code of honor they all lived by in the camp—they all had pledged faithfulness to one another no matter what. The code kept them united even through the toughest times. And at the top of the code was this unwritten assumption: "First in…first to leave."

They understood that whoever among them had been imprisoned the longest, having suffered the longest, should be the first to return home, even if it meant the others might die before being rescued or set free. "There is a friend who sticks closer than a brother," the book of Proverbs says (18:24). These men were that kind of friend and more.

Five other men at the Plantation had been held captive longer than McCain. If he went home ahead of any of them—any of his *friends*—what would that say to those who remained behind?

Craner insisted that because McCain had been so seriously injured, no one would hold it against him if he chose to leave. "You don't know if you can survive this," Craner argued.

McCain was not only weak and sick but also fearful of what would happen if he told his captors no.

Yet it occurred to him that he was being offered freedom only as a propaganda ploy, since his father was a high-ranking officer. (McCain was unaware of a development his captors learned at this time—that his father had just been chosen to command all American forces in the Pacific.) McCain also suspected that his return home ahead of the other prisoners would be used against those left behind at the Plantation. Their captors would try to demoralize these men who had no admiral for a father. They would mock the friendships that once had seemed so strong. "Your *friend* is back home with his wife. Going out to dinner. Lying on the beach. Your *friend* has betrayed you."

Laying Down Your Life

After three days it was time to face the Cat again. McCain declared that he'd thought the offer over carefully. If his friends who had been imprisoned longer than he could accompany him, fine. Otherwise, he wouldn't do anything that might hurt his friends.

His captors exploded in a rage.

"Now it will be very bad for you!" said the Cat.

And it was, as McCain goes on to explain in his book.

Meanwhile, on the very day he refused to go home, his father officially assumed command of the U.S. forces in the Pacific. But all that military might under his command wouldn't save his son from the torture and beatings to come.

John McCain's choice to stay committed to his friends came at an incredible price. For five more years he would have to endure his brutal, terrible captivity. It wasn't until 1973 that he was finally released, along with the last of the prisoners from the Plantation. After a long rehabilitation, McCain resumed his service with the Navy, eventually retiring as a captain in 1981.

It's difficult to imagine a more costly decision to be there for your friends, isn't it? But those are the friendships that most reflect God's love and commitment to us.

Jesus said, "Greater love has no one than this, that one lay down his life for his friends" (John 15:13). John McCain laid down five more years of captivity for his friends; Jesus laid down it *all* for his friends—including you.

What about you? Are you satisfied with the commitment and caring level of your friendships? Do you want to see them grow deeper and stronger? If so, keep exploring with me what it means to be there for others.

5 | *Being There for a World in Need*

Every once in a while, something happens that seems to defy logic, like seeing a movie sequel that's actually better than the original or finding a parking place right near the mall door an hour before closing on Christmas Eve.

We can imagine other events that approach the realm of statistical impossibility. Imagine receiving a letter from the IRS that begins, "We are so sorry, but we made a mistake and here's some money back…" Or a Good Samaritan returning your lost wallet with the cash still in it and not a single credit card missing.

Or teenagers getting up early on Saturday morning to work for free.

Or a huge drug manufacturer giving away expensive medicine to people who really can't afford to buy it.

These last two actually occurred, believe it or not. And through these true-life stories, we can sharpen our focus on what it means to *be there* for our neighbors and fellow citizens of earth.

"Happy Helpers for the Homeless"

Near Baltimore a group of teenagers has decided to be there for some hurting people. They get up early (without cash bribes) each Saturday morning to help people they don't even know. Their leader is a young woman named Amber Coffman.

Amber rates an entire chapter in John Kasich's wonderful book, *Courage Is Contagious*.[1] He tells how Amber always had a soft heart for others. She loved to accompany her mother to Sarah's House, a homeless shelter located on the Fort Meade army base. While her mother taught basic life skills to homeless parents, Amber interacted with the children in these families. Her heart broke as she heard the children tell of being abandoned and unloved.

That's when Amber decided to do something to help the homeless.

"I knew I couldn't put a roof over their heads," she says, "but I wanted to do what I could. I was sure other kids would volunteer if they had a chance. I knew from the first that I wanted to provide meals. And I knew that giving them food wasn't as important as giving them love."

Amber began by raiding her family's refrigerator and making a bag of sandwiches. Homeless people could often be seen a short drive from her neighborhood in Maryland, so along with her mother she drove out of her neighborhood to find them and offer them sandwiches. In the process of handing her sack to a very appreciative, very hungry homeless person, Amber and her mother discovered how meeting another's need could fill their own hearts as well.

And that was only the beginning.

Today, on any given Saturday, as many as forty students from area schools crowd into Amber's modest apartment. Instead of sleeping in or watching cartoons, these volunteers secure hundreds of slices of cheese, some sixty pounds of bologna, and more than six hundred donated hamburger buns to prepare for the next day. Then on Sunday, after attending Heritage Church of God in the morning, Amber, her mother, and her Happy Helpers for the Homeless drive into the poorest sections of Baltimore.

Since 1993, Amber and her friends have fed more than twenty-five thousand men, women, and children and have provided more than six hundred volunteers the chance to be there for others.

What about you? Being there for others may not lead you to make a single sandwich for the poor, but people all around you are hungry for your words or your hugs. They need a mentor in their business or help with their homework. They need you to be there for them.

I challenge you to look around your work, church, school, neighborhood, or city and find the needs that God lights up before you. Hey, if a major corporation can do it, why not you?

A "Drug Dealer" Chooses to Be There

What's the world coming to when even teenagers are learning to be there for others? We can only hope it's becoming more like Merck and Company, a "drug dealer" of the best kind. Its story provides an incredible picture of what a company can do to be there for others.

For more than 110 years, the Merck family has been in the pharmaceutical business. Over those years, Merck has built a thriving, profitable company through its outstanding research and development teams. Merck was the first to synthesize vitamin B_{12} and was credited with bringing cortisone to the market. It has also developed a number of so-called miracle drugs, including the cholesterol-lowering drug Mevacour, which is credited with lowering heart attack rates by 40 percent.

Those drugs all provided tremendous bottom-line success. Yet it's what Merck did with an unprofitable pill that shows how even corporations can be there for hurting people.

Did you know that for almost ninety years, people living near many of Africa's beautiful rivers have been going blind by the time they reached their fifties? Blindness by middle age was considered a given. In many villages, young children lead their elders around.

As early as 1917, doctors and researchers discovered the source of this problem, which is known as river blindness. A fly living in the slow-moving waters that run through infected countries would bite people and leave behind a parasite. That parasite would multiply, and over the course of years, it caused the terrible blindness as well as skin sores.

It maddened doctors that while they knew the source of the problem, they couldn't stop the suffering. Sprays didn't work in eradicating the flies for more than a few days, and no medicine had been developed to kill the parasite once it had begun its deadly work. Medical science could offer no hope to the people infected in those lands. If you were bitten, all you could look forward to was a walking stick with your name on it.

Enter a company with a desire to be there for the suffering.

In 1978, William C. Campbell, a lead research scientist in Merck's New Jersey laboratory, was studying treatments for parasitic worms in livestock. His team was close to a breakthrough medication that would one day be called Ivermectin. After its eventual release in the 1980s, it became one of the world's most potent agents against heartworms and other animal parasites.

As Campbell observed Ivermectin's dramatic effects on a strain of horse worms, he made a life-changing connection. If Ivermectin worked so well in getting rid of *Onchocerca cervicalis* (horse worms), he thought, perhaps a different form of the drug would work against a biological cousin, *Onchocerca volvulus*—the dreaded human parasite that caused river blindness.

Campbell's heart raced as he thought how eighty-five million people at risk in thirty-five developing countries might be protected. And even more, perhaps the eighteen million people already carrying the river-blindness parasite could be helped.

No Payoff?

But all Campbell had was a hunch, an intuition. Armed only with that hope, he went to his boss, Dr. P. Roy Vagelos, and asked for approval to develop a form of the drug for human use.

The potential human benefits seemed huge, but the potential costs to Merck looked staggering. Even without complications, the development of a new drug cost an average of $200 million and twelve years for all the required tests and approvals. On top of that would be manufacturing, marketing, and distribution costs if the tests proved successful. And here's the worst part for a multinational company accountable to stockholders: Even if the company did spend all the time and money and effort needed to create a drug to help river blindness, the people who most needed it couldn't afford to pay for it.

Despite these discouraging realities, Vagelos approved Campbell's study. Why? Because he knew Merck is not merely a drug company. It's a company with a heart to relieve human suffering, a company that strives to be there.

Campbell and a team of experts went to work. They tested more than forty thousand microorganisms before finding the single one that produced the dramatic results they were seeing in animals with Ivermectin.

Clinical trials proved spectacularly successful and safe in treating river blindness. Not only did people's sight stabilize and often improve, but also the constant skin itching that plagued many sufferers completely disappeared. Field tests in Africa proved even more miraculous. To even the most skeptical, it looked as if a cure for river blindness had been found.

To be sure, it had cost Merck three times the $200 million originally projected. But now the company had a pill that cost three dollars to produce, caused almost no side effects, could be administered in a single dose just once a year, and could stem the tide of river blindness.

Only one hurdle remained, and it was a big one: getting the drug to the people who most needed it but couldn't afford to buy it.

Merck approached several governments, but not a single country would help fund the project. There was no payoff, other than curing the sick, in stopping river blindness. Clearly it would be nothing short of corporate nonsense for Merck to produce the pills.

So Merck gave up, right?

Wrong.

Not only did Merck decide to produce the pills at its own cost, but it determined to give away the drug away to anyone who needed it...forever. It even formed a public health group to help at-risk nations deliver the badly needed medicine.

Make no mistake, Merck displayed tremendous courage in putting human need ahead of profit. My wife and I own only a few shares of stock in a few companies, but one of them is Merck and Company. While I'm no financial advisor, I couldn't help but invest in a company that has chosen to be there for people, regardless of the profit.

Merck isn't alone in that distinction, by the way. Over the years I've been privileged to meet and speak for a number of companies, many of whom are Christian corporations doing business alongside secular counterparts. I'm thinking of industry leaders such as Interstate Batteries, Chick-Fil-A, Herr Foods, Citizen's Insurance, and even my publisher, WaterBrook Press.

I realize your job all day may be stamping invoices *Paid* instead of stamping out river blindness. But if you'll be there as God's representative at your work and in your community, you can make a world of difference. Wherever you are, you can live out *Christ's* promise to be there for others—a promise we're now ready to investigate.

PART TWO

Because God Chose to Be There

Our family recently had the rare privilege of seeing a traveling exhibit of the work of Claude Monet, the great French impressionist painter.

We loved it. *All of us.*

The "all" includes a nine-year-old street-hockey player, a teenager who resented having to get up at the crack of noon to go see some "dumb" paintings, my wife who bought the tickets, and the one person in our family who actually thinks those fluorescent Elvis paintings done on black velvet are art. (And yes, I actually owned one…before I was married, of course.)

Despite having tickets to the exhibit at the Phoenix Art Museum, we waited in line longer than we did for the *Star Wars* prequel. By the time we were finally allowed into the museum, I think it's safe to say Mr. Grumpy had invited himself to stand in line with us.

Inside, we each received a headset attached to a tape recorder that would guide us through the exhibit. I teamed up with Laura, our younger daughter, and we pushed the *play* button together. At one very large painting, the articulate voice instructed us to walk right up to it.

Now, to stand within a few feet of a Monet is to see a blur of colors and shapes; every texture and hue seems to collide with the next. Brush strokes arc everywhere, and what look like globs of paint hang helter-skelter on the canvas. At such an artist's-eye view, I was thinking, *We paid top dollar to wait an hour in line...for this?*

But then, coached by the patient recorded voice, Laura and I stepped back several paces. With the change in perspective, our mouths fell open. Instead of an incoherent blur of color and shape and texture, suddenly we were looking at a beautiful pond of lilies. Gorgeous trees like weeping willows marched around the pond, with branches like long fingers lightly brushing the surface of the water. Five steps back took us from a muddle of paint and color to a masterpiece. Even to an Elvis-on-black-velvet kind of guy, the effect was breathtaking.

Laura and I turned to see if Cindy and Kari's experience mirrored our own. It did. We ran toward each other, and in an excited huddle we each swore we could see the wind gently rustling the lilies on the pond.

In a similar way, to grasp the full meaning of the two little words *be there*, you have to take a step back. You can't stare at these seven simple letters, pushed together, and dismiss them as inconsequential or insignificant. You have to step back to see them in context, in the masterpiece that is God's Word.

You've paid for your ticket and waited in line this far—now it's time to push the *play* button on the tape recorder to see what the Bible says is so special about these two words. We'll gaze at the canvas of Scripture and view two unique pictures. Each is a distinct contrast in emotion and purpose and people, and each adds its own foundation, color, texture, and shape to what it means to be there.

Initially, these two events might seem as unrelated and pushed together as the color and texture choices of a Monet viewed nose to canvas. But once we've stood back from each event (by taking apart key words and phrases in the passages), we'll see how they combine to create a landscape that takes your breath away. In the center of the picture that appears, you'll observe a pathway that beckons you into God's garden, a place of sold-out, vibrant, colorful life. A place my mother lived her days and where others like her have learned to "glow" in every season of life. A place where God's Spirit really does move the lilies on the pond.

As we push the *play* button and begin our biblical tour of what it means to be there, I'll be asking you first to step up close to the vibrant, sun-splashed flurry of colors captured in a great celebration. Then we'll see how the contrasting tones and delicate brush strokes of a more familiar portrait are mixed in.

If that sounds like a mess in the making, just wait until we step back and see how these two unique divine pictures work together to display a priceless masterpiece shaped by God's expert hand.

6 | *God Came Near in the Temple*

It began with a great celebration that took months to plan and great effort to pull off, a celebration filled with music and song and sacrifice and the birth of a new level of relationship. It was the greatest of all grand openings. And it's where we begin our quest to see what it means to be there for others.

Why? Because the best way to discover what it means to be there for others is to investigate what God himself did to be there for us. What steps did he take to build long-lasting relationships with his children? How did he connect with his people? What, exactly, did he do to create personal, enduring connections with the men and women he made in his image?

But we can't stop there. After we learn the answers to those questions, we need to go one step further and ask, "How can we pattern our actions after God's model?"

Our ultimate goal in this tour through Scripture is to see how we can learn through God's example to make rich and enduring connections of our own. When we see the way *he* went about building deep relationships with his people, we may begin to understand how we, too, may connect at a profound level with others.

Spectacular Grand Opening

Grand openings are meant to be spectacular. Take the night Planet Hollywood opened on the beautiful San Antonio River Walk. Local police estimated that more than sixty thousand visitors showed up for the restaurant's grand opening. Those hordes weren't coming to sample the appetizers; they were hoping for the merest chance to glimpse their favorite Hollywood stars. And with luminaries like Arnold Schwartzenegger, Bruce Willis, Demi Moore, Tom Cruise, and others rumored to be in attendance, San Antonio police had their hands full in trying to control the crowd.

A throng of sixty thousand men and women standing shoulder to shoulder on the River Walk certainly ranks as a Hollywood-size event. But God's Word describes another grand opening that makes the Planet Hollywood debut look like a family picnic.

No one has ever seen anything like the dedication ceremony that opened Solomon's temple in Jerusalem almost three thousand years ago.

For eight full days and nights, an entire nation converged on the city. Israelites from north and south set up their tents like mobile Embassy Suites while they attended speeches, celebrations, and solemn ceremonies to mark the occasion. So many people came that we're told their tent city stretched from the temple to almost twenty miles south of the city.

Organizers of Planet Hollywood's grand opening served more than 1,000 dinners from their kitchen in a single night. Bruce Willis threw in with a rock band hired for the event, and the night ended with a fireworks show. Pretty impressive!

But nothing could compare to the party God threw.

At the dedication of the temple, King Solomon offered up 120,000 sheep in a single offering—with 22,000 oxen thrown in for good measure.

During the elaborate ceremony, a joyful noise erupted from countless throats, producing a roar like nothing ever heard. Thousands of singers lifted their voices in unison to join the cymbals, harps, lyres, and 120 trumpets, making "themselves heard with one voice to praise and to glorify the LORD" (2 Chronicles 5:13).

Bruce Willis may have brought down the house in San Antonio, but in Jerusalem, after all the singers and instruments finished playing at the dedication of the temple, we're told heaven itself came down!

> Then the house, the house of the LORD, was filled with a
> cloud, so that the priests could not stand to minister
> because of the cloud, for the glory of the LORD filled the
> house of God. (5:13-14)

And if all the sacrifices and music and songs and the cloud of God's presence weren't enough to leave people more awestruck than any Super Bowl halftime show, the ceremony ended with the ultimate in fireworks displays. Solomon closes the eight days of celebration with this simple prayer:

> Now, O my God, I pray Thee, let Thine eyes be open, and
> Thine ears attentive to the prayer offered in this place.
> (6:40)

The dramatic answer appeared at once.

> Now when Solomon had finished praying, fire came down
> from heaven and consumed the burnt offering and the sac-
> rifices; and the glory of the LORD filled the house. (7:1)

Now, *that's* a sight that would make the much-ballyhooed millennial fireworks display atop the Eiffel Tower look like a dozen bottle rockets going off. What an awe-inspiring, earthshaking, emotional event!

And yet…why so much ceremony for the opening of a place of worship? Why throw such a huge celebration? Why sacrifice so many cattle and sheep for a mere building dedication?

The answer is that God was *not* simply dedicating a building. He was initiating a dramatic paradigm shift in his relationship with his people. He intended to show them what he meant when he promised that he would be there for them. And he didn't want them to forget. Ever.

The Security of Settled Roots

In our day—when God's people are his temple, and his covenant with us is written on our hearts, rather than on stone tablets placed in a gilded box—it's easy to miss the significance of this amazing event. But try to put yourself in their sandals for just a moment.

These people had known mostly displacement since the days of Abraham. They were wanderers who longed for a secure homeland. Most of all, they yearned for a place to stop and worship their God without having to pack up and move on the next day. They craved a real connection with God that would remain stable, firm, and deep.

For hundreds of years, Abraham's offspring had languished in Egypt as slaves. Then God raised up Moses to deliver them from captivity, and with a mighty hand the Lord plucked his people out of their misery. At Sinai the Israelites saw the awesome holiness and power of God and heard his command to build an ark of the covenant and a portable tabernacle to house it. But only a short while later, on the very cusp of entering a land flowing with milk and honey, they instead turned back in rebellion and spent the next forty years doing laps around the wilderness.

During that weary time in the desert, their days of journey would begin when the priests picked up the long poles attached to the ark of the covenant and began to walk forward. In the evening, the people camped where the ark was set down. They also took the ark into battle, but they had always carried it by the poles, for they rightly feared to touch it. They pictured the ark as a footstool for God's feet.

During all that time, and even after the Israelites finally entered the Promised Land, the ark of the covenant served as the central symbol of almighty God's presence and his lasting covenant with his people. That would not change with the dedication of Solomon's temple. In fact, archaeological expert M. Pierce Matheney notes, "The primary meaning of the temple was the same as that of the ark it was constructed to enshrine: a symbol of God's presence in the midst of His people."[1]

So after centuries of having the traveling tabernacle as the home for the ark of the covenant, what now changed with the construction and dedication of the temple?

I can answer that in three words:

Permanence.

Stability.

Continuity.

(And just for the record, these happen to be the three crucial elements every human heart craves in its most cherished relationships.)

To establish a *permanent* resting place for the ark was a change at least as dramatic as those that follow a wedding. Remember the relief that swept over you when you finally got married and no longer had to drive across town (or fly across country) to spend time with your beloved? For a nation of wanderers, a close-by, reserved parking place for the ark must have seemed like the end of the rainbow.

God Had a *Somewhere*

At last, God's people had a solid, immovable, tangible *somewhere* for God's ark to rest—right in the very heart of Solomon's temple. In one glorious moment they were ushered into a sense of permanence about their faith that none of their fathers had ever enjoyed. At that moment, they felt more connected to their God than they had ever felt before—a connection so real and tangible that all they had to do was look up at the temple's beautiful architecture or walk over and touch its walls. Once an Israelite had glimpsed the temple doors or felt its stones, he or she knew God's promises were for real. (Orthodox Jews still do this today when they nod and touch their foreheads to the Western Wall, also called the Wailing Wall, the last remaining vestige of the ancient temple rebuilt by Herod.)

Now do you begin to understand the deep connectedness to God that the ancient Jews felt through the dedication of their new temple? It was as if the temple itself were saying to them, "You are wanderers no more. You may live here and put down roots here, for your God lives among you. He will not leave. He will be here tomorrow morning when you arise, and he will still be here tomorrow evening when you lay your head to rest. You are *home,* people of God, because your God has made *his* home right here. Peace now. Rest now. And glory in your new sense of his presence!"

Even in our day, we feel a natural insecurity about the lack of a permanent place to worship. Just ask any member of a start-up church who has spent years hauling sound equipment and children's supplies back and forth between grade schools and empty office buildings. On the first Sunday in the church's very own sanctuary, there are tears, praise, thanks, relief, and most of all, an amazing corporate sense of...

- "Now, at last, we can put our focus on growing deeper in our faith, instead of moving equipment or trying to buy land or finance a building."

• "Now, at long last, we can concentrate on putting down roots."

That must have been the feeling of the nation as ancient Israel celebrated the dedication of the temple. No longer would God's people have to play catch-up with the ark, wandering wherever it went. Now their ark would remain permanently in a beautiful building, and they could concentrate on building a homeland with God's very presence in their midst.

That's why the dedication of the temple was such a big deal to God and to his people. It was like a homeless family signing papers on their very first home (minus the loan papers and termite inspection, of course). For similar reasons, the Pilgrims who founded our country were willing to brave an ocean journey in small ships and then a harsh life in a wild frontier to find a place of their own where they could worship according to conscience.

And that's why, after all the emotion and drama and pageantry and praise and heavenly witness of the temple's dedication, we're told that the people returned to their tents "rejoicing and happy of heart" (7:10). Like a group of fans leaving the stadium after winning a national championship, these people headed back to their tents, packed up for their trip home, and fell sound asleep—all smiles and sweet dreams.

But what of Solomon?

After all that emotion and celebration, he had no way of knowing that the best was yet to come.

Promises in the Night

To get a picture of how tired Solomon must have been after the dedication of the temple, imagine being executive director of the Rose Bowl parade. Your responsibility is pulling together hundreds of people and thousands of details into a glorious, on-time event for millions to watch.

Can you imagine how stressful that job would be, in addition to the incredible drain on your emotional and physical reserves? If so, then magnify that stress level by a factor of eight (days, that is).

After more than a week of directing such a massive celebration, it's easy to picture Solomon falling exhausted onto his couch when he is finally home alone. If anyone deserved a siesta, it was Solomon. If I were him, I'd have hung a "do not disturb" sign on the bedroom door and warned the servants they'd be on the next camel train out of town if they didn't let me sleep in.

But for Solomon, sleep wasn't on God's agenda. We're told that late that night, Solomon received a miraculous wake-up call. In the quiet hours following the big ceremony, there came an unexpected visitor to a tired, emotionally drained man:

> Then the LORD appeared to Solomon at night. (7:12)

It was an unforeseen call that came at just the right time, with just the right message (much like that call made to the father of the bride).

Isn't that just like our Lord? He loves to save the best for last, whether it's wine in Cana or Christ's return in glory. Solomon didn't know it, but the best part of the dedication of the temple wouldn't be the memory of the celestial fireworks show. Instead, it would be the words about to be spoken by almighty God himself. His declaration carried a promise that shows us a great deal about commitment, caring, and deep connections— and what it means to be there.

"I have heard your prayer," God assured Solomon. And he added,

> Now My eyes shall be open and My ears attentive to the
> prayer offered in this place. (7:12,15)

Imagine! God personally awakened Solomon to give him a *yes* answer to his request. With the opening of the temple, God would indeed turn his attention to his people, but not like a boss who grudgingly agrees to meet with his employees after a strike or like a busy school principal who finally opens her door to a group of disgruntled students.

Out of love, not out of obligation or coercion, God would hear his people's prayers and be attentive to their needs. When his people came close to his presence (in this case, when they gathered in the outer courtyard of the temple to pray, near the Holy of Holies that housed the ark of the covenant), he would draw near to them.

Can you imagine a better reason to be awakened? To have the Lord himself nudge you awake and promise you that his eyes and ears would turn toward you?

Without meaning to trivialize God's Word, his promise is like a loving parent saying, "I want you to know I'm all eyes and ears, anytime you want to talk." That's a promise that's only as good as the parent's word. The promise to Solomon was based on *God's* faithfulness, which is complete. The Lord never backs away from promises linked to his character.

The precious words soothed Solomon's weary soul…as well as the soul of a nation. They gave a long-missing sense of security, of lasting commitment, and of unending love. God's words, in fact, were the key to providing a true sense of rest in a time of significant change.

Moreover, God wasn't finished! No sooner had Solomon begun to absorb the magnitude of God's promise than the almighty Lord of heaven and earth gave the king yet *another* promise, this time with his name written all over it. It's a promise more reliable than the Rock of Gibraltar, for it's given by the One who created the Rock of Gibraltar. This is what God told Solomon about the temple:

I have chosen and consecrated this temple so that my
Name may *be there* forever. My eyes and my heart will
always *be there*. (7:16, NIV)

Here's a closeup of the key words translated from the Hebrew text:

Forever,
my name
will be there.
Always,
my eyes and my heart
will be there.

In this amazing promise, God committed himself to be there for his
people in several specific ways. And though in Solomon's day he fulfilled
his commitment through the temple made of stones, in our day he continues to fulfill it through the temple of the Holy Spirit, who lives in our
hearts.

It's time now to turn our attention to each of the remarkable elements
of God's promise to Solomon. As we come to understand what it means
to have God's name and eyes and heart *be there* for us forever and always,
we can begin to see clearly what it means to be there for our loved ones.

7 | *God's Name Is Here*

Parents in King Solomon's day took a very different approach to picking a name for their child than most of us do today. In our culture, the Go-for-the-Famous-Name Syndrome leads many parents to pick their child's name based on someone or something they admire. Unfortunately, that often means rock stars or soap-opera stars—or actual stars. "Hi, this is my daughter, Orion, and my son, Betelgeuse."

Other parents fall into the We-Thought-It-Was-Really-Funny-at-the-Time Syndrome, where they choose a name such as Moon Unit or Buffy or Ima Hogg, knowing full well their child is too young to press charges. Those custom-named kids spend their whole lives looking in vain for a key chain or bike license plate—and often years in intensive psychotherapy when they're grown. (Assuming, of course, they survive the gauntlet of teasing better known as Second Grade.)

Still other parents go with the Spontaneous-Naming Syndrome, where they find a name in a *Top 100 Baby Names* book at the grocery checkout counter, or they both agree that the nice bank teller they just met has the "perfect" name for their child.

In short, parents today tend to look *outside* the child when picking a name. They choose a name that they simply like or that matches the name of a celebrity or successful person or relative they respect. By putting that name on their child, they're hoping their son or daughter will grow up to be like Elvis or Elway or Elmo.

But in Solomon's day, parents went the opposite direction when searching for just the right name—they looked at the child. In Solomon's day, a child's name was chosen to reflect something of that individual's character or essence.

"But," some guy out there responds, "how can you name a newborn to describe his or her character? How do you know *anything* of the child's essence just moments after your little one enters the world?"

Only men would ask something so foolish. Every mother bristles when someone says, "All babies look alike" or "All babies cry alike." They know it just isn't true.

Remember, it was the mother who came up with Jacob's name just after her son was born. Jacob was the younger twin who came out of the womb grabbing hold of his older brother's ankle. His name means "one who grabs hold" or "supplanter"—something that proved true many years later when Jacob stole his brother Esau's birthright and blessing.

In ancient times a child's name, even as a newborn, was meant to showcase something significant about that person. It was like a billboard advertising a unique or important characteristic of the individual.

Can you imagine being named after your character or essence? That would make for some very interesting name-calling if we followed this ancient tradition today.

Imagine if we still picked names based on a person's essence. (I won't even speculate on the names suitable for certain political figures.) What would *your* name be if it represented all you are—your essence? What would people call you if your name reflected the character you demonstrate day by day? Would friends and family call you Faithful? Dedicated? Demanding? Angry? Prayerful? Skeptical? Worried? Scheming? Wonderful?

In the book of Proverbs we're told, "A good name is to be more desired than great riches" (22:1). If our name rings up wonderful memories, positive thoughts, or remembrances of promises fulfilled, our character may be counted as priceless. If, on the other hand, our everyday essence reeks of selfishness or inconsistency or dishonesty, our name isn't worth a deflated dime.

Name = Essence and More

When we understand that in biblical times a person's name represented his essence—and as a result, reflected his character—the promise God gave Solomon concerning his divine name seems all the more amazing and packed with meaning. And it gives us our first look at what it means to be there for others. Here's a paraphrased reminder of that promise:

My name will be there.

When God made this commitment to Solomon, he had but one name in mind, his most holy name, the name he revealed earlier to Moses at the burning bush.

Is it possible for us to fully grasp how astonishing it was for God to put himself on a first-name basis with his people? That's really what happened when God spoke to Moses through the burning bush and directed him to return to Egypt and free the Lord's people.

But before Moses took a single step from herding sheep to gathering a nation, he had a very good question on his mind:

> Then Moses said to God, "Behold, I am going to the sons
> of Israel, and I shall say to them, 'The God of your

fathers has sent me to you.' Now they may say to me, 'What is His name?' What shall I say to them?" And God said to Moses, "I AM WHO I AM"; and He said, "Thus you shall say to the sons of Israel, 'I AM has sent me to you.'" (Exodus 3:13-14)

There's a good reason Moses wanted to know God's name. In biblical times, giving someone your name was a necessary first step in establishing a meaningful connection. In the Hebrew culture, if a stranger came to your home and asked you for food or housing (there being few inns and fewer hotels back then), you were obligated to provide for their basic needs. But *only* if they gave you their name. The principle was this:

No name, no relationship.

When God appeared to Solomon on the night following the dedication of the temple, he could have identified himself through any one of a dozen divine names that appear in Scripture. Yet because he wanted to make sure that Solomon understood the magnitude of his promise, he chose to use one particular name. To ensure that no one would misunderstand his desire to deepen his relationship with Israel, he solemnized his promise by using his most personal of names: I AM—the name Moses heard at the burning bush.

That name was considered so personal and sacred to the Jews that they wouldn't even write it out fully or speak it aloud for fear of showing disrespect to the Almighty. So jealously did they guard the private, personal name of God that in time it became a mere huddle of consonants, YHWH. Whenever someone read Scripture aloud, they would substitute the name *Adonai* ("Lord") in place of *Yahweh*.

And it is *that* most holy name that God himself pledges will be there for his chosen ones.

- The Lord God who is faithful to all his promises—that God will *be there* for his people.
- The Lord God who extends his peace like a river—that God will *be there.*
- The Lord God who gives life to the dead—that God will *be there.*
- The Lord God who lives in the blinding excellence of perfect holiness—that God will *be there.*
- The Lord God who judges and makes war—that God will *be there.*
- The Lord God who delights in mercy—that God will *be there.*
- The Lord God who calls things that are not as though they were—that God will *be there.*

All There

Are you beginning to see the magnitude of the promise God gave to Solomon—and, through him, to his people? When the Lord promised, "My name will be there," he meant that everything he is and everything he stands for would be there for his people. When God puts his name on something, he commits all of himself—all his desires, all that he wills, all that he represents and all that is dear to his infinitely loving heart—to that most blessed of places.

When God promises to put his name somewhere, he means that the One who calls himself I AM WHO I AM will be there, *all* there, just for you. And not on video, but in person and in full color.

That means no surrogates.

A few months ago when I walked into a church to do a seminar, a lady approached me in shock. "I can't believe it's really *you*," she exclaimed. "I thought this was a video seminar!" That's the thing today; often you can't be sure if the event is going to be "live" or on tape.

But there was no mistaking the Lord's message to Solomon.

The God of heaven declared unilaterally and unambiguously that "My" name will be there. Not "I'll send one of my people to talk with your people." Not "My associate's name will be there." Not "My angel's name will be there."

No, God promised, "My name will be there."

What a wonder this is! The name above all names; the name that makes seas to boil and the skies to fall; the name that causes every knee to bow and every tongue to confess—that name and all it represents would be there for the people of God. On that remarkable night so long ago, God himself swore that all his character and all his essence would surely be there for his children.

But what does this mean for us?

It means we can count on the One who parted the ocean and calmed the seas to be there for us when the opposition bears down at full speed or the storms of life toss us around like plastic cups caught in the surf. The very essence of the One who lifted up the mountains and raised up the dead will be there to lift us up to new heights and to raise us up with his Son on the last day. The sum of all God's character and power and authority and holiness—100 percent of everything about him—will be there for you and me.

That's a staggering thought and promise. It's enough to chew on for a while, don't you think?

But in your chewing, don't wander away just yet. There is more—much more—to God's promise than the presence of his name. We've just peeked into his character.

So it soon will be time, in the next chapter, to look deep into his eyes.

But first, I have a something personal for you to consider.

A Personal Application Project

Welcome to the first and, without a doubt, the most important reflective assignment in this book. I want to ask you the most important question you'll ever be asked (or one day have to answer):

Do you have Jesus' name on you?

I'm not talking about wearing a Christian T-shirt or putting a bumper sticker on your car. What I want to know is this: Is Jesus' name written on your heart?

A lot of people don't know that, one day, everyone who loves Jesus will "wear" his name. We learn about this in the very last book of the Bible (the book of Revelation), in the very last chapter. There the apostle John is given a guided tour of what eternity will look like:

> And he showed me a river of the water of life, clear as crystal, coming from the throne of God and of the Lamb.... And on either side of the river was the tree of life...and the leaves of the tree were for the healing of the nations. And there shall no longer be any curse; and the throne of God and of the Lamb shall be in it, and His bond-servants shall serve Him;

And here it comes:

> And they shall see His face, and *His name shall be on their foreheads.* (22:1-4)

Wouldn't you like to find the well of life that can quench your most raging thirst? Or pick a leaf from the tree of life that can heal hurts as deep and wide as any war or ethnic dispute that now rips apart nations?

Wouldn't you like to step out from under the curse fully cleansed and washed and pure of heart, like the first hot shower after a summer week spent in the woods?

Most of all, can you imagine gathering with the multitudes of the world who loved Jesus, from every generation and tribe and nation, right in front of God's throne? There you would find total acceptance, rest, and a task that brings utter fulfillment in serving him.

And there, too, you would see Jesus face to face. Your eyes would drink in that Friend and Counselor and Encourager and Savior who has been calling you to himself all these years.

Heaven will be a place where people proudly wear his name—the name above all names, Jesus. The name that can live in your heart and be the wellspring of an abundant, fulfilling life today—and eternal life forever.

So let me ask you once again: *Do you have Jesus' name on you?*

If it's not already, it can be. If you'd like to make a reservation today for that wonderful scene the apostle saw in Revelation, there is an invitation with your name on it right here.

The apostle Peter, speaking of the blessed name of Jesus, declared, "And there is salvation in no one else; for there is no other name under heaven that has been given among men by which we must be saved" (Acts 4:12).

The apostle Paul made it clear how that name saves us when he quoted the prophet Joel: "Whoever will call upon the name of the LORD will be saved" (Romans 10:13).

If you want to put on the name of Jesus right now, just pray the following prayer. As you pray, know that Jesus is true to his Word, because his name is I AM.

Dear heavenly Father,

Thank you so much that you've given your Son to be my Savior, Redeemer, Counselor, and Friend. Thank you that for everyone who comes to you in faith, your name will be there, both now and forever. Thank you, Lord, that through the mystery of your Holy Spirit's working, praying a simple prayer like this causes time and eternity to meet in this present moment.

Lord, I ask you to forgive my sin—all those times I've fallen short—and I ask you to come into my heart and guide my steps and guard my heart. I love you, Jesus, and I want to wear your name and live my life to love and bless and honor you. I thank you so much that you've promised to never leave nor forsake me, that you will always be there for me in the days to come, even through endless days in heaven.

I love you, Jesus.

Amen.

If you've just prayed that prayer, *congratulations!* All of God's promises about being there are absolutely true…and absolutely for you.

8 | *God's Eyes Are Here*

In his commitment to Solomon, almighty God promised more than that his name would be there.

My eyes and *my heart* will be there.

This sentence in 2 Chronicles 7:16 is the only time in Scripture where God's eyes and heart are so closely linked. So while it's obvious that these two are harnessed together and run neck and neck, in this chapter, we'll let the "eyes" have it.

This part of God's promise implies action. Simply put, he sees a need with his divine eyes and has the compassion of heart to do something about it.

A New Way of Seeing

What does it mean that the Lord's "eyes" will be there for us? Perhaps it will help to consider what the space shuttle *Endeavor* accomplished in a recent earth-mapping mission.

Less than ten hours after blastoff, the shuttle astronauts deployed a 197-foot radar antenna mast from the ship's cargo bay. Like a huge, collapsible fishing rod, 87 stacked cubes made of steel, titanium, and plastic were cranked out by a small electric motor, one section after another extending into space. Attached to the foremost section was a 26-foot radar antenna that, when fully extended, spread out like the top-cross on a *T*.

As *Endeavor* orbited 145 miles above the earth, another 39-foot antenna secured in the cargo bay beamed radar signals at the earth. The twin beams swept across the planet in a swath 140 miles wide and bounced back into space, where they were received by both the cargo-bay antenna *and* the antenna 197 feet away at the tip of the mast. By combining the two sets of data, scientists were able to triangulate an image and thus secure the information necessary to compile 3-D snapshots of our world's terrain. The result: unprecedented accuracy and clarity for mapmakers.

Impressive technology, yet NASA still lags infinitely behind God's perfect view of us.

Think about it: "Are not two sparrows sold for a cent?" Jesus asked. "And yet not one of them will fall to the ground apart from your Father. But the very hairs of your head are all numbered. Therefore do not fear; you are of more value than many sparrows" (Matthew 10:29-31).

Imagine how long the mast on the space shuttle would have to be to map the hairs of your head. (No fair if you're follically impaired.) Perhaps that comparison can help you to see how personally and intimately the Lord watches his own.

God's eyes see the details of our days, whether they're filled with sorrow or celebration. His eyes are there for us when we move to a new city and don't have a single friend. We never send our children to school without his eyes locked on them every moment. He closely observes his own day and night, for "Even the darkness is not dark to Thee, and the night is as bright as the day. Darkness and light are alike to Thee" (Psalm 139:12).

We can get a good picture of just how carefully and intensely and thoroughly God's eyes sweep the earth when he watches over us by noting the sorts of things God perceives from his throne high in heaven.

- He sees when we are cheated, as Jacob learned: "I have seen all that Laban has been doing to you. I am the God of Bethel" (Genesis 31:12-13).

- He sees when we are oppressed, as the people of Israel learned: "And the LORD said, 'I have surely seen the affliction of My people who are in Egypt'" (Exodus 3:7).

- He sees when we are rebellious, as Moses learned: "And the LORD said to Moses, 'I have seen this people, and behold, they are an obstinate people'" (Exodus 32:9).

- He sees when our sin has made us sick, as Isaiah learned: "'I have seen his ways, but I will heal him'...says the LORD" (Isaiah 57:18-19).

In fact, God's eyes pierce the blackest night and cut through the thickest fog with zero loss of clarity. He sees all, and he sees it all at once and perfectly. As the New Testament declares, "All things are open and laid bare to the eyes of Him with whom we have to do" (Hebrews 4:13).

In order to see like that, with infinite and minute and exacting detail, God's eyes never grow passive. They're always on search mode. Like the antenna in the space shuttle's cargo bay, God's eyes are always scanning the earth to see whom he can support. The Bible says it like this: "For the eyes of the LORD move to and fro throughout the earth that He may strongly support those whose heart is completely His" (2 Chronicles 16:9).

God delights in using his eyes to map out how he can support us— how he can be there for us. That alone is a wonderful, incredible gift.

The Best Reward

When you fly into Phoenix these days, it's hard to look down and find a house without a backyard pool. These days, pools seem to be the only things here that outnumber Starbucks coffee shops.

But that wasn't the case when I was growing up. Not only were we missing a backyard pool, but we were also missing a neighborhood pool (or a swimming hole anywhere nearby). That is, until a small pay-to-swim facility opened up a few miles from our home.

Perry Pool.

On red-coil summer days, we'd all meet Mom at the door when she got home from work and beg her to take us to Perry Pool. Of course, for us boys the real heat suffering was all our own; forget that Mom had just driven for almost an hour—without air-conditioning—from downtown Phoenix where she worked. *We* were the ones melting like microwaved M&M's.

Many were the days she agreed to take us to the pool, despite being hot and tired after a full day's work. Cheers would echo down the hallway as we'd sprint to our rooms and grab our suits. Every second counts when you're a kid who gets to go swimming. Mom would change into shorts, grab the towels that always drooped like sleeping possums on the clothesline, and toss both towels and boys into the backseat of her Ford Falcon.

I guarantee there was more energy bouncing on the backseat of that car as we headed to the pool than ever was created by the engine that powered it. I even hate to use the word *power* in the same sentence with our three-on-the-tree Ford Falcon. It had to be the slowest car ever made. In all my childhood, I have no memory of actually passing another car that wasn't parked—and I have plenty of embarrassing memories of motorists honking at us to speed up when Mom already had her foot to the floor.

Within milliseconds of our arrival at Perry Pool, we were in the water—

not just because of the excitement of swimming, but because this was long before any kind of cool deck was invented. The concrete around the pool always burned lava-hot, and that meant we had to dash across the fiery cement, jump high in the air, and hang there for a split second before splashing down into Perry Pool's cool, refreshing water.

We'd sink slowly to the bottom of the pool, not moving a muscle, determined to stay there, engulfed by all that chilly liquid, and never face the heat again. That is, until our air ran out and we'd reluctantly bob to the surface, smiling and luxuriating in the blue depths…

Until the *games* began.

After thirty seconds of bobbing, three very competitive boys are no longer content merely to swim. They want to compete. And while we played many games in the pool, they all had one element in common. They all started and ended with the words, "Watch me, Mom!"

There was the initial jump into the water that always required her eyes. And then the diving and big splash contests she had to judge. And of course, the I-bet-I-can-hold-my-breath-longer-than-you double-dare contest that *demanded* her eyes be on us the entire time (or we'd surely drown).

But most of all, I remember diving for quarters.

You see, as an advanced arthritic, my mother never was able to get in the pool and swim with us. Although the water would have felt wonderful to her hot joints and body, the steep steps down into the pool became a roadblock. She might have gotten in, but there was no helping bar as in today's special-needs-friendly pools. And there was no patient, caring husband to take her by the arm and lift her out. So she'd sit in the sun or find what shade she could and watch her boys swim. (Funny how she never complained about sitting on that baking concrete while we had so much fun in the pool.)

Diving for quarters was just like it sounds. The three of us boys would scramble out of the pool and shake the water from our crew cuts (the official haircut of young boys in the summer). Then, one at a time, she would toss three quarters into the water, and each of us got to play frogman and dive in to rescue them.

For hours it seemed—until her arm would finally wear out—we'd play fetch the quarter. It was always the same. When it was our turn, we'd stand on the side, muscles tensed, watching intently to see where the quarter plopped in, then dive in at the splash and swim like mad past the bubbles, just in time to see a shimmering flash. It was the quarter, our prey, wiggling toward the bottom like a depth charge. We'd swim furiously underwater, then finally stretch out like an all-star outfielder to try to catch it before it hit bottom. Sometimes we'd even succeed. But every time, whether we caught the quarter before it hit or not, we'd plant our feet on the bottom, push up and rocket toward the sun, a quarter-clutching fist the first body part to break the surface.

Then it was time for the awards ceremony.

Only our reward wasn't the quarter. We had to give *that* back. (Quarters were precious in our house in the fifties).

Neither was our reward the air. (Even though those deep-end dives could be trying.)

The reward was...*her eyes.*

Her eyes would always lock onto ours as we burst to the surface. She always looked impressed, as if somehow we'd just brought up an Olympic gold medal or dug up a Spanish doubloon instead of the quarter she'd dug out of her old brown pocketbook.

Her eyes being there for us were the reward—and in them we found the attention and love and value that three father-starved boys needed more than trophies. Her eyes, full of love, felt better than pool water on scorching summer days. Her eyes, like God's eyes, searched and found us and said we were much more than okay. We were special and valuable and loved. We were somebody worth being there for.

Crew cuts and all.

Perfect Eyesight

We gain so much when someone important really *looks* at us. It means the world when a person we respect views our game, watches our graduation, sees our wedding, witnesses the birth of our child, notices where we live or work. We long for a loved one's eyes to be there for us when we're scared of the surgery we're facing. We delight when someone we admire sees our thrill at the promotion we earned on our first real job.

And that is precisely what God promises to do for us. When he swears by his own name that his eyes will be there, he is guaranteeing that he will continually watch over us, look out for us, *see* us. And in seeing perfectly, he will take perfect action.

During all the years since God spoke to Solomon that night long centuries ago, and for every year to come, the eyes of almighty God have been there for his own. They will keep on counting sparrows in the sky and hairs on your head—even if you're losing some or they're turning gray—because the smallest detail of your life and of all his creation is valuable to him.

Now, stop to ponder that for a moment.

Isn't it mind-blowing that the God of the universe actively enjoys watching the details of your life? He sees your bad days and lousy attitudes—and still loves you. He sees the shallowness and the times you stretch the truth to look better than you are—yet when you finally look up in shame, you see forgiveness in his eyes.

So does our God look only for the sin in our lives? Does he carefully observe only the mistakes we make?

No way! God is delighted to see all that we do *well*.

His eyes light up when he observes us completing a project or when we choose not to share that great bit of gossip or when we turn off a pathetic television show or when we spend time reading the Bible or reciting a story to our kids.

Every time we do something well, even if no one else sees it (or ever will), his eyes—which have been searching, scanning, probing, just waiting to catch us doing that right thing—affirm and encourage and support us. By fastening his eyes on us, he wants us to feel that we've just earned a gold medal in the Olympic stadium of heaven.

God delights in seeing his children do well. Can you imagine the joy in our Lord's heart when he inspired the following reports to be written in his eternal Word?

- "Asa did what was right in the sight of the LORD, like David his father" (1 Kings 15:11).
- Amaziah "did right in the sight of the LORD" (2 Kings 14:3).
- Hezekiah "did right in the sight of the LORD, according to all that his father David had done" (2 Kings 18:3).
- Josiah "did right in the sight of the LORD and walked in all the way of his father David, nor did he turn to the right or to the left" (2 Kings 22:2).

You can almost hear the mighty choirs of heaven belting out loud praise songs as the anonymous scribes who wrote those words set pen to parchment. It pleases God to no end when he sees us do well.

I know, of course, that many of us tend to focus on the negative. We're prone to remember all the times the Bible uses the phrase "And so-and-so did evil in the sight of the LORD." And it's true that this discouraging phrase shows up in Scripture much more often than its positive counter-part. God, after all, always tells the truth.

But do we really suppose that God *likes* to observe us messing up? Do we think it gives him any pleasure to see us doing evil in his eyes?

Rather, isn't it wonderfully true that our Lord rejoices when we do well? Didn't he himself ask his people, "'Do I have any pleasure in the death of the wicked?' declares the Lord GOD, 'rather than that he should turn from his ways and live?'" (Ezekiel 18:23).

God's great heart bursts with joy when he observes his children doing well. He celebrates to see each of our spiritual victories, just as all heaven rejoices when one sinner comes to repentance.

That's how God's eyes look at us through his Son, Jesus. He watches us, studies us, and observes us closely that he might instruct us, correct us, protect us, guide us, encourage us, and help us to become increasingly more like his Son.

What awesome delight we're privileged to give our Lord through his eyes! It's a delight that goes straight to his *heart*—which just happens to be what we'll investigate next.

9 | *God's Heart Is Here*

You'd been planning your "dream vacation" for months. Two dozen visits to the library, five consultations with top travel agents, three transatlantic phone calls, and uncounted hours on the Internet all worked together to help you create the perfect itinerary.

You bought the right tickets.

You made the right reservations.

You secured the right amount of traveler's checks.

Then you counted down the days and hours until you and your beloved would board the plane and head off to paradise.

That's why you're not the least bit prepared when, five minutes before you lock the doors and head off to the airport, your honey hits you with, "Babe, I don't think I want to go after all. My heart's just not in it."

At that moment, what rips through your mind? If such a thing ever happened to me, I imagine several thoughts might explode inside my fevered brain:

- *Your heart's not in it? Then get a transplant. RIGHT NOW!*
- *So leave your heart at home—but your body's coming with me!*
- *Any more heartless comments like that, and you'll give me a heart attack.*

No doubt several other choice words would also quickly surface, but

I trust you get the idea. When your heart is fully into something and you think the heart of your beloved beats in sync with your own, it's quite a shock to hear, "My heart's just not in it."

You thought her thinking jibed with yours. *It didn't.*

You thought he felt just like you did. *He didn't.*

You thought she had chosen what you had. *She hadn't.*

When two hearts that should beat as one instead pound out contrary rhythms, the result can be…well, heartbreaking.

But just imagine what happens when the heart of your beloved really does thump to the same cadence as your own…when your thoughts and emotions and will correspond exactly with his or hers…when you know beyond a shadow of a doubt that even if your loved one didn't thrill to the same dream vacation that enchanted you, he or she would delightedly accompany you anywhere—because his heart, her heart, belonged completely to you.

It makes a world of difference to know where someone's heart really and truly lies.

And that's why we ought to rise up and shout an earsplitting *Amen!*—because God assures us that his own heart will always be there for us.

Heart = Intellect, Emotions, Will

You'll find the word *heart* in the Bible a measly 667 times. When it isn't describing the pump beating in our chest, it stands for three things all at once: the intellect, the emotions, and the will.

When someone's heart is "in" something, biblically speaking, that person's intellect, emotions, and will are 100 percent present and accounted for. All that person's thoughts, feelings, and choices are certain to be there. No questions. No compromises. No chance of slippage or decay.

On the night God stood before Solomon and said, "My heart will be there," our Lord meant that 100 percent of his mind, feelings, and will would be bent toward his people. They would have his attention—all of it. They would arouse his passions—all of them. They would see his determination—every bit of it.

You see, when God's heart is in something, it's all the way in. And his heart is "in" his people!

But what does this mean, practically speaking? How does God connect with his people through his intellect, emotions, and will? When he told Solomon that his heart would be there for the people, what exactly did he mean?

Let's take a quick tour through Scripture to get a better picture of how God's heart beats for his children.

The Mind of God Thinks on Our Behalf

We're told that God's thoughts are without number and are as high above our thoughts as the heavens soar above the earth. That's the prophet's famous proclamation in Isaiah 55:8-9. But how sweet it is to realize that a large chunk of our Lord's innumerable thoughts focus on you and me! I love *The Living Bible* paraphrase of Psalm 139:17-18, a song of David:

> How precious it is, Lord, to realize that you are thinking
> about me constantly! I can't even count how many times a
> day your thoughts turn towards me. And when I waken in
> the morning, you are still thinking of me!

David never got over that awesome realization, and neither should we. But exactly what kind of thoughts does God have about us? What is he thinking about all the time?

For one thing, he's thinking about how to instruct us. As Nehemiah said to the Lord, "Thou didst give Thy good Spirit to instruct them" (Nehemiah 9:20). We need that instruction to know how to do his will and enjoy his blessing and success. So God himself says, "I will instruct you and teach you in the way which you should go; I will counsel you with My eye upon you." (Psalm 32:8).

God also is thinking about the dangers that lurk all around us. To enable us to avoid them he gives careful warnings. He cries in Psalm 81:8, "Hear, O My people, and I will admonish you; O Israel, if you would listen to Me!" He gives these warnings because he knows what hazards lie ahead. On the road we're traveling, he sees the bridge that's been washed out up ahead, even if we can't.

And he's thinking about his plans for us. "'For I know the plans that I have for you,' declares the LORD, 'plans for welfare and not for calamity to give you a future and a hope'" (Jeremiah 29:11). They're plans we can trust, because "the counsel of the LORD stands forever, the plans of His heart from generation to generation" (Psalm 33:11). His plans for us come straight from his heart of love for us.

What a gift to know we never have to worry whether God is thinking about us, because he always is.

The Emotions of God *Feel* on Our Behalf

Certain philosophies and religions give many people the false impression that God is aloof and distant, that he's uncaring or cold-hearted toward us, or at best neutral.

But that's all wrong. God is not apathetic toward us. When he says his heart will be there for us, he means that his emotions and feelings overflow their banks every time he considers us (which is all the time).

You can hear it between the lines in passages like this one, as he cries out to the people who have spurned his loving attentions:

> How can I give you up, O Ephraim?
> How can I surrender you, O Israel?...
> My heart is turned over within Me,
> All My compassions are kindled.
> I will not execute My fierce anger;
> I will not destroy Ephraim again.
> For I am God and not man, the Holy One in your midst,
> And I will not come in wrath. (Hosea 11:8-9)

God's attitude toward his people is never halfhearted. It's all-hearted. His feelings are totally involved. To show us that, Scripture records God as being "grieved" or "angry" with his people, as well as "pleased" and "joyful." He sings over his beloved (Zephaniah 3:17, NIV) and he laughs at his enemies (Psalm 2:4). He is never an unfeeling God.

God sees our need and our pain and always reacts emotionally. As perhaps the best picture of this, just think of the simple statement the gospels give us of Jesus with Mary and Martha at the graveside of Lazarus: "Jesus wept" (John 11:35).

The truth is, God feels more deeply than we could ever imagine.

The Will of God *Chooses* on Our Behalf

It's the same story when we look at how God exercises his will on our behalf. We owe everything to the choice and loving will of God. We're his chosen ones. He has told us, "I've chosen you." And if we asked what would happen if he had to do it over again, the answer would be, "I would choose you."

In Scripture we see our heavenly Father making his children feel chosen. Take the time he lined up the nation of Israel and told them,

> For you are a people holy to the LORD your God. Out of all
> the peoples on the face of the earth, the LORD has chosen you
> to be his treasured possession. (Deuteronomy 14:2, NIV)

Did you know that's how almighty God feels about you? That you're chosen above all others and are his "treasured possession"? That should do wonders for your view of yourself on those days the boss unloads on you or a traffic cop gives you a ticket. It may seem as if the world is against you, but your heavenly Father chose *you* to love.

We also see God's choice of his own in the way Jesus handpicked his disciples. "You did not choose Me," he tells them in the Upper Room just before his death, "but I chose you, and appointed you, that you should go and bear fruit, and that your fruit should remain" (John 15:16).

Jesus chose to give them his name—to invest in them his time, counsel, correction, love, and commitment. And his choice to love them (and us) wasn't simply an afterthought. We're told, "He chose us in Him before the foundation of the world, that we should be holy and blameless before Him. In love He predestined us to adoption as sons" (Ephesians 1:4-5).

God chose us in love.

What a comforting, inspiring, humbling thought.

In his eyes, there are no accidents or oversights. As King David said to God, "For Thou didst form my inward parts; Thou didst weave me in my mother's womb" (Psalm 139:13). The knowledge that the God of the universe chose before we were born to bless us and love us—and even suffer and die for us—can overcome any hurt...if we'll just let his love in.

God's loving heart, which he promised would be there for us, constantly chooses to act on our behalf, to do whatever is necessary to connect with us—even when his hand is not apparent.

When God promises that his heart will be there for us, he means that he is committed with every ounce of his omnipotence to exercise his will on our behalf. He chooses to connect with us, and he always will.

Always. Has a nice ring to it, doesn't it?

It's even nicer when it pours from the mouth of God, which it does. Let's look at that next.

A Personal Application Project

It's time for another personal assignment. I promise you it's sweeter than a dozen Krispy Kreme doughnuts that have just rolled by on a conveyor belt and are handed to you in a box while they're still hot.

Do you know the difference between a *translation* of the Bible and a *paraphrase?* If you don't, don't feel bad. For years I didn't know either. The answer is that a *translation* is basically a word-by-word rendering of the Bible (like the King James translation or the *New International Version* or the *New American Standard Bible*). An English translation is an attempt to be very accurate in matching what's in the original languages of the Bible (Hebrew, Greek, and a little Aramaic) with the right English word. But in a *paraphrase,* a language scholar is trying to capture the broader intention or ideas behind the original phrases and restate them in English. A paraphrase is more of an idea-by-idea rendering (like Dr. Ken Taylor's *Living Bible* and Eugene Peterson's *The Message*).

I wanted to make that distinction because I want you to read part of Psalm 103 in paraphrase form. A paraphrase is an attempt to get at the heart of what God is saying in a passage, and this passage from *The Message* says so much about God's heart. (Guess who wrote the original? Someone whom God said was a "man after his own heart"—King David himself. Who better to show and tell us about God's heart?)

So in your best easy chair or just before bed or surrounded by the steady hum of an airplane engine or after you've parked your car and before you go into work, enjoy reading about God's heart:

Psalm 103—A Paraphrase

Oh my soul, bless [Yahweh].

From head to toe, I'll bless his holy name!

Oh my soul, bless [Yahweh],

don't forget a single blessing!

He forgives your sins—every one.

He heals your diseases—every one.

He redeems you from hell—saves your life!

He crowns you with love and mercy—a paradise

crown.

He wraps you in goodness—beauty eternal.

He renews your youth—you're always young in

his presence.

[Yahweh] makes everything come out right;

he puts victims back on their feet.

He showed Moses how he went about his work,

opened up his plans to all Israel.

[Yahweh] is sheer mercy and grace;

not easily angered, he's rich in love.

He doesn't endlessly nag and scold,

nor hold grudges forever.

He doesn't treat us as our sins deserve

nor pay us back in full for our wrongs.

As high as heaven is over the earth,
    so strong is his love to those who fear him.
And as far as sunrise is from sunset,
    he has separated us from our sins.
As parents feel for their children,
    [Yahweh] feels for those who fear him.
Men and women don't live very long;
Yahweh's love, though, is ever and always,
    eternally present to all who fear him.

10 | *A Forever Kind of Presence*

Words like *forever* express a wonderful sentiment and always show up on plaques at places like Cracker Barrel. But in real life, the word *forever* poses a distinct problem for people living during the "dash" years—the years lived in the dash on our gravestone, between the date of our birth and the date of our death.

Understanding *forever* wouldn't be such a problem if we weren't such finite people. So fragile. So terribly prone to just up and die. Even things around us that once seemed so stable—like jobs, marriages, Charlie Brown and Snoopy, and most of the companies I've bought stock in—can be gone in the blink of an eye.

Being handed a concept like *forever* is like handing a one-year-old a regulation-size basketball. The child may have all the desire in the world to grasp it, but his pudgy little fingers and hands just aren't big enough to hold it for long. And even when he hugs it close and tries to carry it somewhere, his arms don't begin to stretch around it.

Yet finite beings can still get a glimpse of *forever*—if we know where to look.

Through All Our Days

Twice in the promise almighty God gave to Solomon in his after-hours appearance, he spoke an identical Hebrew word. Now, whenever God uses the same word repeatedly in the same passage, you ought to sit up and take notice, because it's important.

That's especially true in this case.

The term here is a compound word that could be literally rendered, "for all days" or "through all days." In its first appearance in the passage, the NIV translates it "forever," and the second time, "always." But the thought remains the same in each case. God says of the temple, "My Name [will] be there *forever*. My eyes and my heart will *always* be there."

So, for how long would God be there for his people?

Forever!

Always!

Through all our days.

God promised Solomon by an oath that his name and eyes and heart would be there for his people *perpetually*.

This *forever* word in 2 Chronicles 7:16 is one that, according to one biblical scholar, "reminds us powerfully that God is present at every moment in time and thus is with us constantly."[1]

Such a potent promise can make a world of difference to someone who is facing new challenges, a scary future, or an unknown adversary. General Joshua faced all those uncertainties as he prepared to take over for a great leader, Moses, and guide the Israelites into the mysteries of the Promised Land.

Was he fearful? You bet. That's why the soon-to-be-deceased Moses told his old friend, "Be strong and courageous, do not be afraid or tremble at them [the Canaanites], for the LORD your God is the one who goes with you. He will not fail you or forsake you.... And the LORD is the one who goes ahead of you; He will be with you. He will not fail you or forsake you. Do not fear, or be dismayed" (Deuteronomy 31:6,8).

Still, the butterflies in this untested leader's stomach didn't quiet down, so God himself later declared to Joshua, "No man will be able to stand before you all the days of your life. Just as I have been with Moses, I will be with you; I will not fail you or forsake you" (Joshua 1:5).

And he never did.

When God says *forever* and repeats it with an *always,* he means business. When he says that his name and his eyes and his heart will be there for his people *forever,* he wants us to understand that he will *never* leave us nor forsake us.

But some may think, *Well, that was a promise to Joshua. It was a promise to Solomon and the Jewish people. I don't think it applies to me today.*

But the New Testament repeats these very words to believers in Christ today. The writer to the Hebrews reminds his church-age audience, "He Himself has said, 'I will never desert you, nor will I ever forsake you,' so that we confidently say, 'The Lord is my helper, I will not be afraid. What shall man do to me?'" (13:5-6).

And if that weren't enough, how about the words of Jesus Christ himself? At the end of Matthew's gospel we read his welcome promise, "Lo, I am with you always, even to the end of the age" (28:20).

God so wants to establish a real and vital connection to us that, through Christ, he has chosen to put his name on us; he has fixed his eyes on us; he has given us his whole heart—and he has done so permanently, through all days, always, *forever.*

I know it doesn't always *feel* like that, but it's still true. That's why the apostle Paul tells us, "For now we see in a mirror dimly, but then face to face; now I know in part, but then I shall know fully just as I also have been fully known. But now abide faith, hope, love, these three; but the greatest of these is love" (1 Corinthians 13:12-13).

When all the smoke and mirrors that make up our fallen world fade away, only what has been faithful and hope-based and loving will remain. But why is love the "greatest" in this trio of faith, hope, and love?

It's because faith and hope are along-the-way words, not end-of-the-trip words. Faith and hope get you through the too-long car trip. They're the looking-forward part that keeps us going until we finally get home. But when at last we pull into the driveway and reach our final destination, the sign above the door will carry a single word: *love*.

The apostle Paul in his beautiful description of *forever* love in 1 Corinthians 13 describes it this way:

> Love never fails; but if there are gifts of prophecy, they will
> be done away; if there are tongues, they will cease; if there
> is knowledge, it will be done away. (13:8)

Committed, *forever* love is the air we'll breathe in eternity one day in heaven. Here on earth, God's type of forever love is the most lasting, stable investment we can make in another person's life or experience in our own. Perhaps that's why the times someone has communicated to us that they'll "be there forever" never seem to leave us. They live in our memory like…like a "tale as old as time," a "song as old as rhyme."

Beauty in the Beast

When you live in Phoenix, you can count on August days that engulf you with oven-strength heat and demand extra-strength sunglasses. Escaping into the cool respite of a movie theater is a wonderful retreat, even if you can't always count on there being something worth watching.

So one afternoon several years ago, Cindy and I loaded up Kari and Laura in their car seats and drove over to pick up my mother to see a movie. For her, being invited to see a movie was like being asked to dance. Her voice filled with excitement when we called, and her eyes lit up when we all showed up at her door. But getting her into the minivan made it a lot like slow dancing. First came the slow parade by walker to our car, then moving even more slowly to help her into the front seat.

When her legs finally were picked up and gently swung around, I hurriedly shut her door and picked up a more staccato beat as we raced to the theater. Then back to slow dancing as we all helped get her into her wheelchair. (Malls aren't walker-friendly to those with surgically replaced knees and ankles.) Finally out of the car and situated in her wheelchair, she opened her arms wide and two of her granddaughters—who had waited with all the patience of heated corn-kernels—popped into her lap for the free ride inside.

I'll never forget pushing the three of them into the theater that day. Mom's little plastic American flag, taped to the side rail of her wheelchair, waved proudly. That wheelchair became the flagship of our family armada in our voyage to escape the heat by seeing *Beauty and the Beast*.

Our family doesn't get overly bothered if we're late getting to a theater, because the front row (seldom filled) has always acted like a magnet to our children. They migrate there whenever their mother lets them. That day, front-row seats were nearly all that remained, and the kids couldn't believe their good fortune. Cindy got the girls settled with their drinks and popcorn a split second before the lights dimmed and the previews began. Meanwhile, I headed for the end of the last row and slid Mom into the place where the seat was missing (reserved parking for the handicapped). I pulled up the lever that locked her wheels and took the seat next to her.

From our vantage point at the very back of the theater, we could see rows of children's heads barely protruding above the seat backs, interrupted occasionally by a grownup's head and shoulders sticking up like feathers on a cap. That afternoon we saw lots of animated kids as well as a beautifully animated love story.

As *Beauty and the Beast* played out, my first inclination was to think of Cindy, sitting down front with the girls. How she's seen beyond my thrice-broken nose and that front tooth that badly needed replacing. How she's looked past my seventies big hair and extra-wide sideburns, and especially past elements of my unsavory past. Somehow, despite all my flaws, she has loved me for what I could become.

But as I sat in the back row and held my mother's hand, I saw how Mom, too, had a huge part in the story. How she had prepared me for the day I would meet Cindy by telling me a thousand times how much potential I had…how handsome I was…what a great husband and father I'd be…how that paper I handed her with the C-minus was just that day's grade—there were lots of A-pluses to come.

Who cared that her words came at a time in my life when teachers were saying that my potential lay in washing dishes…when I struggled with acne…when I knew I came from a long line of men who had walked away from their families.

Mom saw the beauty in the beast. Why? Because she had determined to see me through heaven's eternal lens.

So had Cindy.

That's the difference that forever can make. We must never forget that our Savior chose us before time began, and that even "while we were yet sinners" he chose to die for us.

Once he's forgiven and redeemed and restored us and replaced all the missing pieces lost to a fallen world, then we're ready to spend forever with him. Forever in a place with no tears, no sickness, no arthritis, no wheelchairs.

It's a place with no beasts at all…just beauties who are finally reflecting his image.

A Personal Application Project

My family has a favorite dessert called Death by Chocolate. It's seven layers of different types of chocolate, all laid down in seven scrumptious thicknesses of moist light and dark cake. It got its name because it truly is to die for. What I'd like you to taste in this assignment has fourteen layers and an incredibly sweet taste; it also has no calories and is especially good for your heart.

It's the fourteen ways the Bible translates the word *forever.*

As you read through the following list of what *forever* means, start by putting your own name in the blank of each sentence. Imagine Jesus himself waking you up late one night and filling your heart with what he means by *forever.* See if all the ripples caused by letting these fourteen words wash over your mind and heart don't lift you up and float you toward a new perspective on the ocean of God's deep, forever love for you.

Imagine Jesus saying to you…

"I will love you, _____, *all the way.*"

"*As far as your life takes you,* _____, I will *always* care for you."

"I am *completely* committed to you, _____."

"*Forever,* _____, I will be there for you."

"It's you and me, _____, *forevermore.*"

"*So long as* you need me, _____, I'm here for you."

"My love for you, _____, isn't measurable; it's *unfathomable.*"

"You can *always* call on me, _____."

"*From ancient times,* I have known the good and bad of your life story, _____, and I will always love you."

"*Continually* I have my eye upon you, _____."

"For *eternity*, _____, I will be there for you."

"I have loved you, _____, with an *everlasting* love."

"I will not forsake or desert you, _____, but will love you permanently."

After you've put your own name in each blank, go back and insert a loved one's name. Better yet, go and find him or her, or pick up the phone right now and call, and read the list aloud. When you do this for your loved ones, you'll be handing them a slice of *forever* for their hearts.

"*Forever*," says the Lord, "*My name will be there.*"

11 | *God Is Here for Us in Jesus*

In the last few chapters, as you've pondered the words God spoke to Solomon just after the dedication of the temple, perhaps a question has sprung up.

It's wonderful that God promised he would be there forever for his people, with his name, his eyes, and his heart intimately attached to the Jerusalem temple.

But wait a minute—there seems to be a big problem here.

There's no temple today.

Solomon's temple was destroyed by the Babylonians in 587 B.C., and the rebuilt temple of Jesus' day was razed in A.D. 70 by the Romans. There hasn't been a Jewish temple since then.

Sure, there's the Western Wall, thought to have been constructed from the ruins of the ancient temple. But in fact, "No stone is left that archaeologists can confidently say belonged to the Solomonic Temple."[1]

So do you see the problem? If the promise God made to "be there forever" was given in the context of a temple that no longer exists—is the promise still valid? And even worse, if God promised that his name and eyes and heart would be there forever, yet the "there" no longer "is"—what kind of *forever* is he talking about?

If Solomon built his temple around 967 B.C. and it was destroyed in 587

B.C., then this worship center stood on Mount Zion less than four centuries…hardly "forever" by anyone's standard.

Is God's idea of forever radically different from our own? And if it is, what sort of comfort is *that?*

God's House

Those are good questions. Tough, but good. And as we'll see, the answers come in a Person who took on the function of the temple.

But before we get to that, let's clear up a few important points about God's promise to Solomon concerning the temple. Bear with me as we dip into a little history; you'll soon see why it's so very important.

On the surface, it looks as if God's promise to Solomon is *unconditional,* that is, dependent upon nothing but God's unchanging, holy character. "I have chosen and consecrated this temple so that my Name may be there forever," he had said. "My eyes and my heart will always be there" (2 Chronicles 7:16, NIV).

Looks pretty cut and dried, doesn't it? But when you read on, you also hear the Lord say this:

> But if you turn away and forsake the decrees and commands I have given you and go off to serve other gods and worship them, then I will uproot Israel from my land, which I have given them, and will reject this temple I have consecrated for my Name. I will make it a byword and an object of ridicule among all peoples. (7:19-20, NIV)

That's as much a promise as the precious words we've been lingering over—and as we just noted, God fulfilled this darker promise *to the letter.*

And yet even though the Lord eventually rejected Solomon's temple, he never did discard his people. In fact, to show the Israelites his determination to be there for them, in 520 B.C. he once again directed the nation to build a place for his name. By this time the ark of the covenant had mysteriously disappeared from history, but God still instructed his people to rebuild the temple, calling it "My house" (Haggai 1:9). This rebuilt temple stood for almost five hundred years, until King Herod began building his own temple in 19 B.C.

This third temple is the lavish facility described in the Gospels. Work on it continued until A.D. 64, and even though it was built by a non-Jew (King Herod), Jesus acknowledged its legitimacy by twice calling it "My Father's house" (Luke 2:49; John 2:16). He also connected it directly to Solomon's temple in three of the four Gospels.

When Christ got out his whip one day and ejected the merchants who had overrun the temple grounds, he shouted, "It is written, 'My house shall be called a house of prayer'; but you are making it a robbers' den." (Matthew 21:13). The verse he quoted is found in Jeremiah 7:11—a verse written while Solomon's temple was still standing. In Jesus' mind, the temple of Herod and the temple of Solomon stood on equal footing.

So much for continuity. But something was about to happen that would change everything forever.

From a Holy Place to a Holy Person

The Gospels describe a time of huge transition, from Old Testament to New Testament, from an emphasis on law to a focus on grace. And at the center of everything is Jesus Christ.

When our Lord told his disciples that all the magnificent buildings of the temple were about to be destroyed, they could hardly believe it

(Matthew 24:1-2; Mark 13:1-2; Luke 21:5-6). How could God abandon his covenant people?

The answer was, he wouldn't. But he *was* getting ready to replace a symbol with the real thing.

The book of Hebrews insists that the Jerusalem temple was never anything more than "a sanctuary that is a copy and shadow of what is in heaven" (Hebrews 8:5, NIV). In fact, it says, the law itself "is only a shadow of the good things that are coming—not the realities themselves" (10:1, NIV).

After Jesus was crucified for our sins, the "copies" and "shadows" would no longer be needed, because the reality had at last arrived. No longer would the temple sacrifices of bulls and goats be required to enter God's presence, for now the perfect sacrifice of his Son had been made.

Jesus' final two statements from the cross were, "It is finished" (John 19:30) and then, "Father, into Thy hands I commit My spirit" (Luke 23:46). At that moment, at the very second he died, the veil that separated the Holy of Holies from the rest of the temple was torn in two, from top to bottom—proclaiming that access to God was never again to be sought through the symbols and the shadows, but through the reality. As the writer of Hebrews explains:

> Therefore, brothers, since we have confidence to enter the
> Most Holy Place by the blood of Jesus, by a new and living
> way opened for us through the curtain, that is, his body,
> and since we have a great priest over the house of God, let
> us draw near to God with a sincere heart in full assurance
> of faith. (10:19-22, NIV)

Even before his crucifixion, Jesus tried to explain that he himself was God's permanent replacement for the temple. "Destroy this temple, and in three days I will raise it up," he told some religious leaders who questioned his authority (John 2:19). Of course, they didn't understand what he was talking about.

> The Jews replied, "It has taken forty-six years to build this temple, and you are going to raise it in three days?" But the temple he had spoken of was his body. After he was raised from the dead, his disciples recalled what he had said. Then they believed the Scripture and the words that Jesus had spoken. (John 2:20-22, NIV)

The point is, all of the Bible's promises regarding access to God and personal, intimate connection to the Lord are fully and ultimately fulfilled through Jesus. A temple in Jerusalem would no longer serve any useful purpose for those in Christ, because full access to God and personal connection to him are freely gained through the living Son of God—not through a building made with hands. That's why the writer of Hebrews, who penned his letter sometime before the destruction of the temple in A.D. 70, could write that the old covenant was "obsolete and growing old" and "ready to disappear" (8:13). That's why he could say that the "gifts and sacrifices" offered at the temple were "only a matter of food and drink and various ceremonial washings—external regulations applying until the time of the new order" (9:9-10, NIV).

And that "new order" is spelled J-e-s-u-s.

Gone But Not Missed

Who needs a temple when you have Jesus? Who needs an ark of the covenant when you have the Lord of Glory?

The Bible contains a lot of profound mysteries, but I think one of the most intriguing questions is this: *Whatever happened to the ark of the covenant?*

As far as Scripture is concerned, it simply disappears. One moment it's in the temple, right where it should be, and the next, nothing. It's just gone. At some point before the Babylonians invaded Israel and destroyed Solomon's temple, the ark simply vanishes from God's Word. No clues about where it went, what happened to it, or anything else. It just disappears.

Except for one curious mention.

The prophet Jeremiah puts on his seer's glasses and looks ahead to a time in the far distant future when Israel will be resettled in her homeland after a long absence. "In those days," the Lord says through the prophet, "when your numbers have increased greatly in the land...men will no longer say, 'The ark of the covenant of the LORD.' It will never enter their minds or be remembered; *it will not be missed,* nor will another one be made" (Jeremiah 3:16, NIV).

Are you *kidding?* I can understand, maybe, why another ark wouldn't be made. But "it will not be missed"? We're talking about the center of ancient Israel's worship. How is that possible?

It's possible because the ark, central as it was, was only a symbol, a shadow. Jesus is the reality, and what intelligent person would exchange a mere symbol for the living reality? What top gun would choose a balsa-wood glider over a state-of-the-art, multimillion-dollar jet fighter? What real-estate broker would choose a Monopoly-game title to Park Place over the genuine article in Manhattan? What eager astronaut would choose a computer simulation over a once-in-a-lifetime round trip to the moon?

No, Jeremiah knew what he was talking about. Who would miss the ark once they came face to face with Jesus? Everything the ark and the temple foreshadowed, Jesus *is.* Everything they pictured, he *embodies.*

Let me show you what I mean.

In Jesus, His Name Is There for You

It was wonderful that God promised his name would be there at the temple for his people—but what if you were a businessman who often traveled far from Jerusalem? What if you were taken captive and sent away into a distant pagan land? If you couldn't get to the temple, how would you benefit from its special status?

All such worries are erased in Jesus.

In him, we have instant access to the Father, no matter where we are or what has happened to us. One of Jesus' names is *Emmanuel,* which means, "God with us." When by faith we confess Jesus as Lord and believe that God raised him from the dead, he takes up residence in our very bodies. "Do you not know," asks the apostle Paul, "that your body is a temple of the Holy Spirit, who is in you, whom you have received from God?" (1 Corinthians 6:19, NIV).

We have no need of a temple made of stones, because God lives within us through Christ. "Christ in you, the hope of glory," as Paul puts it in Colossians 1:27. Jesus has so identified with us through his holy name that we are called "heirs of God and fellow heirs with Christ" (Romans 8:17).

Jesus insists that all he is and all he has will be there for you and me, just as certainly as his name is Emmanuel.

In Jesus, His Eyes Are There for You

Have you ever wondered why the Lord Jesus saw people so much differently from others?

Everyone else saw a short, ill-tempered, cheating tax collector who was polluting the tree he climbed in order to get a glimpse of Jesus. But in

Jesus' eyes Zacchaeus was not scum, but someone who needed to have dinner with the Son of God.

Everyone else saw a woman caught in the act of adultery, a woman who needed to be stoned. Jesus saw a group of accusers who needed to look first at the sin in their own lives.

A whole group of mourners saw grieving parents who had lost their precious little girl. They laughed at Jesus when he said he saw a sleeping girl, not a dead one. Whose eyes saw best? Jesus raised her up and gave her back to her joy-struck parents.

It's as if Jesus looked at people and life around him through 3-D glasses that others just didn't have.

Jesus saw people differently because his eyes didn't merely look on the outside of a person's life. As Ken Gire points out in his wonderful book *Windows of the Soul,* Jesus didn't look only through the window of their life, but past it to their deepest needs, hurts, and dreams.

He embodied the truth of 1 Samuel 16:7—"The LORD does not look at the things man looks at. Man looks at the outward appearance, but the LORD looks at the heart" (NIV).

Jesus saw past the surface because he was determined that his eyes would be there for his people. And you know what? In all the years since he walked the roads of Palestine, his vision hasn't dimmed the tiniest little bit.

In Jesus, His Heart Is There for You

You don't know much about a loving heart until you've seen Jesus in action.

The Gospels paint a portrait of Christ that in essence defines what a loving heart really is. Everywhere he went, the Master proved that his heart would be there for his people.

Jesus' *intellect* constantly challenged and encouraged and amazed his listeners. He instructed the crowds in the way of God, using parables to connect with the common people. He provided for the needs of his followers, sometimes directing them to a coin in a fish's mouth, sometimes multiplying loaves and fishes to feed hungry thousands. Having warned his disciples about "the leaven of the Pharisees," he also warned the Pharisees about mistaking outward appearances for inward reality. He planned for the time he would leave his band of disciples, charging one of them to step up to leadership and directing all of them to wait in Jerusalem for the empowering of the Holy Spirit. Knowing what awaited him, Jesus counted the cost of his mission to earth and willingly suffered a criminal's death.

Jesus' *emotions* spilled over into everything he did. He cried at the death of a friend, and he wept over hard hearts rushing toward judgment. He grew deeply troubled as the hour approached for his betrayal, and he gave thanks, full of joy, that his Father had willed to reveal the identity of his Son to little children. His anger burned at self-righteous religious leaders, and his compassion overflowed for the sick and the destitute.

Jesus could not simply look at misery and choose to do nothing. When he saw crowds full of people captive to ignorance and disease, Matthew says, "He felt compassion for them, because they were distressed and downcast like sheep without a shepherd" (Matthew 9:36). His be-there heart prompted him on the spot to heal "every kind of disease and every kind of sickness" and to preach to them "the gospel [good news!] of the kingdom" (9:35).

Ultimately, Jesus' *will* made him into the Savior he is. He freely chose to come to earth, become a man, and live as an impoverished son of Abraham for more than thirty years. He chose to submit himself to his parents while he was growing up, and he chose to submit himself to his heavenly Father throughout his time on earth. "I have come down from heaven, not to do My own will, but the will of Him who sent Me," he declared in John 6:38.

He exercised his will continually for the benefit of those he came to save. When a leper fell to his knees before Jesus, begging him that "If you are willing, you can make me clean," the Savior reached out his hand, touched the leper—which no one ever did—and replied, "I am willing.... Be clean!" (Mark 1:40-41, NIV) Instantly the man was healed. And when the time approached for Jesus to begin his march to the cross, he assured his disciples that "For this reason the Father loves Me, because I lay down My life that I may take it again. No one has taken it away from Me, but I lay it down on My own initiative" (John 10:17).

When we gaze at Jesus' heart, we quickly become convinced that here is a Person who can be trusted when he tells us he will always be there for us. The only time Jesus ever described his own heart, he called it "gentle and humble"—and offered that as the supreme reason we can feel secure in coming to him for rest (Matthew 11:28-29).

Never an Orphan

In the Upper Room at the Last Supper, just hours before Jesus was handed over to the Romans for execution, the Savior's thoughts centered on his followers, not on the tidal wave of suffering that even then roared toward him. After telling his disciples (again) that he was about to be taken from them, he immediately moved to quiet their alarm.

"Do not let your hearts be troubled," he told them. "Trust in God; trust also in me. In my Father's house are many rooms; if it were not so, I would have told you. I am going there to prepare a place for you. And if I go and prepare a place for you, I will come back and take you to be with me that you also may be where I am" (John 14:1-3, NIV).

In his last hours with his closest friends, Jesus acted decisively to settle unsettled hearts. "Don't imagine that this is it," he was saying. "The story won't be over with my crucifixion. Far from it. In fact, that's just the beginning. I must leave you physically for a little while, but that's only so I can prepare your permanent living quarters. You're coming to stay with me! And when I return to pick you up, we'll never be parted again."

In the meanwhile, he promised that he would never leave them "as orphans." Though he would soon depart earth physically, the Holy Spirit (whom he called "the Comforter") would soon be "in" them. Through the Spirit, Jesus guaranteed that "I will come to you" (John 14:17-18).

In other words: "You'll never be alone. I'll never abandon you. I've promised I'll be there for you *forever*—and I keep my promises."

And just in case any of them might have forgotten, the last thing he said to them before being taken up into heaven was, "Surely I am with you always, to the very end of the age" (Matthew 28:20, NIV).

That means *forever.*

That means *eternally.*

And that's a be-there promise that never quits.

Beyond all types and symbols and shadows, Jesus is the ultimate example of what it means to be there with one's whole heart. He lives out wholehearted love, and he does it every moment of every day. To look at him is to see clearly what being there is all about.

And now the trick is to emulate the example we see.

PART THREE

How to Be There for Others

Have you ever been to an IMAX theater or seen a specially formatted movie where you had to wear those incredibly stylish 3-D paper glasses—the ones with the blue and red plastic lenses?

The afternoon our family went, it looked as if a hundred celebrities had tried to sneak into the theater unnoticed by wearing cheap shades. Since the glasses are so cool, everyone pops them on as soon as they've grabbed a seat. But all you see when you look around is a blur of red and blue. That's because 3-D glasses don't bring things into sharp focus until the screen lights up and the specially formatted film begins.

But once the action starts, those 3-D glasses really work. Without them, watching a shark movie still keeps you in the relative safety of your seat. But watch that same movie in 3-D at the IMAX (as we did), and razor-sharp teeth are snapping only inches from your nose. Their tails almost brush you as they swim past.

You simply don't get the full picture if your eyes aren't equipped to see in 3-D—and that's just as true in real life as it is in a movie theater.

That's because reality is 3-D, not 2-D. Without observing life in 3-D, we miss much of what's really going on around us. We fail to see the needs for security and love that are crying out to be met in those who live and work near us.

In order to live out what it means to be there, it's as if God has asked us to walk around with special 3-D glasses—just as Jesus did. When we do so, it's amazing how God lights up the screen right in front of us, showing us person after person whose needs and fears and hopes we may have walked right by.

God wants us to look with Jesus' eyes. At your family. At those you're driving past on the way to work. At those at work around you. Look to see if they have a need you can meet. How can your name be there for them? How can your eyes be there for them? How can your heart be there for them? And how can you let them know you will be there for them unconditionally?

Who can you see differently today, now that you've got on those special 3-D glasses that Jesus wore?

The incredible thing is that God really can give us his eyes and his heart. As he promised that his name will always be there for us, so can our names always be there for others.

So let's put on those glasses and see how this works...

12 | *Being There for Your Kids*

From the very first moment of birth, children cry out for someone to be there for them. A newborn boy's tiny fingers and chubby arms reach out to be held. A miniature mouth involuntarily sucks the air, searching for her mother. Quivering lips let out a precious cry for the lost warmth of the womb.

With all the trauma and exhaustion of traveling through the birth canal and into a brand-new world, babies who are wrapped up in a blanket and placed in a loving parent's arms often fall fast asleep. Despite all the tactile and temperature changes, the bright lights, the unfamiliar sounds and smells, attachment overcomes anxiety. Having someone be there brings a deep sense of rest.

What's true for newborn babies becomes even more true for preschoolers and grade-schoolers, high-school kids and college-age young adults. In fact, at any age, knowing that your parents chose to be there for you is a wonderful blessing. It gives you a deep sense of being centered and secure, a potent feeling of being connected in an increasingly disconnected world.

But what does it look like to be there for a child?

That's what we'll consider in this chapter and the next as we investigate what it means to have our name and eyes and heart be there always for our children.

Finger Painting the Words *I'd Choose You*

A few years ago, I had the privilege of speaking at a Christian Medical and Dental Society gathering in Colorado Springs. Several hundred physicians and their spouses attended, and Cindy and I had a great time with some of God's special healers. But one couple in particular left a lasting impression on our hearts. We were drawn to them by the touching story of their son, Danny, whom they were helpless to heal.

Both the husband and wife in this family were doctors. They approached me after one session to say how much a book I'd written had meant to their son.

I'd Choose You is a children's book about a little elephant named Norbert. The pachyderm's day begins very badly, but it radically improves when he finds out something wonderful after getting home from school. His parents tell him that out of all the kids in the world—including the flamingo who's a champion ice-skater, the rhino who's not afraid to jump off the high dive, or even the caterpillar who will grow one day to be a butterfly—his parents chose him. *I'd Choose You* became Danny's favorite book, and his parents wanted me to know why.

When their son was only six years old, they were both far away at a medical conference. Simultaneously each of their beepers went off—an emergency page from the boy's baby-sitters. Danny had begun to run a high fever, and the couple watching him was requesting instructions. These doctor-parents immediately called a pediatrician friend who made some suggestions and even called in a prescription. But the illness would take more than that.

The young boy's fever shot up so high and so quickly that the baby-sitters finally rushed him to a local hospital. Doctors were finally able to bring Danny's temperature down and save his life, but the fever robbed him of his hearing in both ears.

Our hearts went out to this couple as they described how guilty they felt for not being there the day their son fell ill. How helpless they felt, even with all their medical knowledge, to keep him from losing his hearing. But through the tears that followed, they thanked God for sparing his young life—and then they brought tears to our eyes as well.

After the fever took little Danny's hearing, it became obvious that this couple would need a way other than spoken words to communicate their love and commitment to their son. So they all learned sign language together.

"The reason we wanted to thank you for the book," they told us, "was because it was always Danny's favorite before he lost his hearing. And when we went to the speech pathologist to learn sign language together, the first words we had her teach us were *I'd choose you.*

"We wanted him to hear those words again from us."

The Dannys of this world, hearing impaired or not, all need to have the silence broken in their lives with those three wonderful words, *I'd choose you.* Each child needs to hear he or she is chosen, imperfections and all. They need to know that Mom and Dad are proud their child wears the family name.

As parents, our job is to let our kids know that our name will always be there for them. They must be convinced that everything we are and everything we have, we choose to use for their benefit. And it all begins with making sure they know we have chosen them.

Does your own son or daughter know that you have chosen him or her?

Just as God chose each of us in love, so also he calls us as parents to be there for our kids by making sure they know they're chosen, that they bear our name. Our name must be there for our kids, just as God's name will always be there for us.

Assurance at the Low Point

The same is true for our eyes and our heart being there for our kids. My mom's eyes and heart were always there for us, and she'd never let us forget that fact.

A dramatic memory surfaces. Late one night my mother and brothers and I were all sitting around the dining room table. Not because we were pretending to eat dinner at midnight in New York, but because the police had just brought us home for being out beyond curfew and for being rowdy.

I remember sitting shamefaced, looking down at the table. And I remember mumbling, "I guess this means you won't love us anymore."

That's when I saw my mother blow up at my words like a whole fireworks factory going up at once.

"I will *always* love you!" she roared.

Her words snapped my head up like a jolt to the chin. With her gray-green eyes riveted on me, she declared, "I will *always* love you...but I am tremendously disappointed in you."

Even then, at the Death Valley low–point of my rebellious days, I knew she meant it. I knew that even though she would ground us and be terribly disappointed in us and struggle to sleep that night (and the next) from worry over us, she really would love us *forever.*

And like never before, that thought—that promise—sank in.

I was loved *forever.*

No matter what kind of trouble I got into.

No matter where my roaming feet would take me.

No matter how I was transported back home.

Mom would *always* love me, and she insisted that I know it.

The Difference It Makes

I am living testimony to what can happen when a parent chooses to fully be there for a son or daughter. When moms and dads decide to be there with their name, their eyes, and their heart, life changes.

Dry, lifeless deserts burst into bloom. Black holes change into stars radiating with bright light. The blind begin to see, the deaf begin to hear, and the dead get up and walk.

Don't think for a moment that's an exaggeration; from my perspective, that's an autobiography. And don't think, either, that my mom could pull off what you never can. She was special, no question about it, but what made her special can also characterize you. You, too, can learn to be there for your kids in a way that will make them bloom, shine, see, hear, and live.

Let me give you a few tips on how to make it so.

It All Begins with a Choice

Four key factors can provide internal checkpoints for parents and grandparents who want to be there for their children and grandchildren. (The same four checkpoints will also help us to be there for our spouse, friends, and community.)

Being there for your child means:
Choosing to connect with him or her...
Being alert in the present moment...
Meeting a need or making a positive contribution...
Regardless of the cost.

Dr. Nick Stinnett is perhaps the nation's leading clinical researcher in identifying what makes strong families. Beginning at Oklahoma State University and continuing at the University of Nebraska, Stinnett and his colleagues have compiled the largest database on strong families in the world.

After interviewing thousands of successful families, Stinnett and his associates have isolated six consistent marks of a *Fantastic Family* (the title of a very good book Stinnett has cowritten with his wife and Joe and Alice Beam). Guess which trait of a strong family is number one on their list?

Choosing to make an unconditional commitment to each child.

In Stinnett's words,

> Members of strong families are dedicated to promoting each other's welfare and happiness. They express their commitment to one another—not just in words, but through choosing to invest time and energy. Their commitment to each other is active and obvious.[1]

To be there as a parent means purposely choosing to invest time, energy, money, and love—hallmarks of commitment that will help each child in the home to feel committed to and chosen.

After I spoke at a conference on the need of a child to feel chosen by a mom and dad, a teacher showed me two letters. She carries these letters in her purse as a reminder of the two types of children she has in her class—and of the kind of letter she wants her children to be able to write one day. I'd suggest getting a tissue handy if letters from young children tend to tug at your heart.

Each letter was written by a third-grader in response to a class assignment. Each child was to write a letter to his or her dad, along with a hand-drawn picture, that would become a Father's Day present.

The letters were written on that beige paper with big lines they give you in grade school. Here's the first letter, unedited for spelling, grammar, and punctuation.

> Dear Dad,
>
> I love it when you take me on dates! I like it when you play baseball with me, miniature golf with me, And watch movies with me. I really aprisheate it! I like it when you read to me at night. I like it when you tell jokes to me. I like it when you take me to school. I like it when you hug me and kiss me. Daddy, I love you!

Now, that's a child's-eye view of a father who's been there for his daughter. It's also the kind of letter any father would like to frame and hang up inside his heart forever.

But that's not the kind of letter the majority of third-graders are writing these days.

That's because half of our schoolchildren are growing up with a father absent from the home and, too often, absent from any significant part of their lives. Far too many children write letters like the following one. The teacher told me the children who wrote the two notes sit just four seats away from each other, but in terms of having a father be there for her, the second child sits a thousand miles away. Again, her letter has been left unedited for spelling or grammar.

> Dear Daddy,
>
> I love you so much. When are you going to come see me agen? I miss you very much. I love it when you take me to the pool. When am I going to get to spend the night at

your house? Have you ever seen my house before? I want
to see what your house looks like. Do you? When am I
going to get to see you agene?

I love you, Daddy

This second letter may bring back painful memories of a father or
mother who wasn't there for you. You may have been victimized by that
loss of connection—but you don't have to stay a victim. You may have
been hurt by the indifference of an absent parent—but you don't have to
pass that same hurt down to the next generation.

Even if your earthly father or mother never showed up at your house,
there is a way to experience love and deep acceptance and to know someone will be there for you forever. You can experience all this in a loving
relationship with your heavenly Father—and experience it doubly when
you pass that love down to your kids. Remember, God has specially chosen to always be there for you. And he calls you to make the same choice
for your child.

A Tragic Letter

I ran across a wonderful book recently that features letters and keepsakes
mailed between loved ones during the chaos of World War II. They're col-
lected in a book titled *I'll Be Home for Christmas*.

It's almost impossible to read the letters from the men in the front lines
without a lump in your throat. (Several letters were received after the news
arrived that a son or father or husband had been killed in action). Yet there
was one letter—actually a poem—that I found particularly tragic.

Not tragic in the sense that a son didn't come marching home (or sail-
ing home, in this case). But tragic in that it shows how generations of

chances to be there for a child can be missed. Oh, how we need to put into words our love or counsel or prayers! Too much goes unsaid when so much is at stake. Here's the poem:

> You stood there, Son, in your navy blues,
> With your cap kinda over one eye,
> And I know that I didn't say very much,
> Maybe just, "Chin up, and goodbye."
> But I've pondered since then, should I have talked to you,
> About cautioning on wrong and observing the right?
> And, Son, my thoughts drifted back twenty-five years,
> And the day I thought me a man;
> Your grandfather there shook my hand,
> And said, "Goodbye, my son."
> So I wonder if he thought, as I left for France,
> Of advice that would not come.
> So, now my hope is that Mother and I
> have been as capable in that way…
> That because of my Dad, just "Goodbye, Son,"
> Was enough when I saw you go.[2]

Those words, first published in the December 1943 edition of *The American War Mother,* typify the deep desire of many parents to "say something" to their child…yet it somehow never happens. Even when the child is standing right in front of them—at a train station going off to war or at a boat dock ready to ship overseas—we fail to say what we could have in the present moment. Somehow he hope that our values or counsel or concern will nevertheless be clearly understood by our child. We hope that "Goodbye, Son" will be enough.

It isn't.

As someone who grew up not hearing those words of love or counsel or concern from a father—and as someone who has counseled hundreds of people with parents of my father's generation who never spoke up—I feel I have ample emotional evidence to declare that unsaid words and a curt "Goodbye, Son" are not enough.

That is, not if you want your children to know that you will be there for them in the present moment.

Good-bye simply isn't enough. Your child needs to know what's in your heart, and he or she needs to hear it in the present moment. Don't live with the regret of wishing you had said something. Don't put off for some vague time "later" when you can speak the love and concern and counsel in your heart.

Do it in the present moment. Do it now, while there is still time, before the present becomes a distant past. Speak the words your child needs to hear or write them down as a keepsake.

There really is no time like the present.

Meet a Need or Make a Positive Contribution

Did you know that the only food that does not spoil is…honey?

Or that Coca-Cola was originally…green?

Or that polar bears are…left-handed?

Or that the average life span of a major league baseball is…seven pitches?

Now, unless you're planning on going for the Trivial Pursuit championship or a spot on *Jeopardy*, you really don't need to know any of these facts. But to be there for your children, to meet their needs or make a positive contribution to their life, you need to know them. Deeply. Intimately. On far more than a trivial level.

God has given Cindy and me two precious daughters who are so different that about the only thing they have in common is the same set of parents. It's not that they don't look alike. Physically they came from the same cookie cutter, but their distinct personalities cause them to approach life from very different directions.

Kari is bold and outgoing, a wonderful leader who meets a new best friend every trip she takes or down every hallway she turns on campus. Laura is a wonderful student who builds best friends into whom she pours herself, and while she's a good athlete, she loves to read and lie back and look at the clouds.

In every home, children are their own book whom we need to read.

My mother had to leaf through the pages of three very different personalities in order to best be there for each of us boys. There was the sensitive older brother who at times felt shoved aside with all the attention people lavished on the twins. There was the detailed, studious younger twin who wanted to be a doctor from the time he was six, and the older twin (by seven and a half minutes), who was more of a party waiting to happen. Each biography looked like it had the same cover, but the contents were startlingly different.

Who in your home has God given you to love and bless and be there for? How well do you know them?

Several years ago, printing magnate Harvey McCay wrote a best-selling business book called *Swim with the Sharks without Getting Eaten,* in which he explained the secret of his success.

McCay explained that he built lasting (and profitable) bonds with his clients by understanding who they were. He knew their likes and dislikes—even their children's names and *their* likes and dislikes.

Isn't that going a little overboard?

McCay doesn't think so. For example, for several years he had tried without success to find business for his envelope company in Japan. He targeted one company in particular and pitched what he thought was a great business plan. He had not built a relationship with the buyer, however, and he was politely turned away.

Frustrated, McCay went back to what had worked for him here in the States, the McCay 66 Questionnaire. He began seeking to understand this man's company and who he was as a person. Soon he discovered this man's daughter loved tennis.

While he's not positive this turned the tide and got him the account, the two tickets to a prestigious tennis tournament that he sent to the man and his daughter certainly made him stand out from his competitors. McCay knew not only what kind of envelopes the man needed but also what would encourage the man's children.

And they weren't even his kids.

At the end of the chapter I'll give you an assignment to help you get to know your kids better. It may not assist you in gaining a new client, but it should do something far better: give you the information you require to meet a need or make a positive contribution to the lives of your kids.

Maybe you'll even take up tennis.

If space permitted (which it doesn't), I would go into detail here on two final things that are crucial to making a positive contribution to your children:

- loving discipline
- the importance of meeting your children's deepest need, namely, sharing your love for Christ.

If you need specific help in discipline, I urge you to read the book *Who's In Charge Here?* by my friend Robert Barnes.

For meeting your children's deepest need, I urge you to join the Heritage Builder campaign, launched by Focus on the Family, to help you gain the tools and skills necessary to become the spiritual trainer in your home.

Without a doubt, helping one's child come to Christ is the greatest gift a parent can provide. It's also the greatest joy we parents can receive, to know that we'll see our kids in heaven. Don't let a day pass without contacting Focus at 1-800-A-Family and asking the good folks there to send you information on the Heritage Builder program. Cindy and I are using the Heritage Builder resources ourselves with our own children, and we know they can be a great encouragement and challenge for many families.

Be There Regardless of the Cost

Robert Weygand was a Rhode Island landscape architect.

He had just finished a $34,000 proposal to do work in Pawtucket's Slater Memorial Park—a project his company needed to "make it," and a project the city was ready to sign off on.

And then the mayor called him in.

The mayor made small talk, then turned up the volume on a nearby radio. Briault said, "I want you to bump up the contract by five—three thousand dollars for me and two thousand dollars for you."

Weygand was taken back by the blatant bid-rigging going on in the mayor's office. But what could he do? If he refused, he knew he would be blackballed on further city work...and the company badly needed this contract to make payroll and pay off debts. Plus, if he went public, would anyone believe him? It would be his word against a trusted public official.

But then three pictures came into his mind.

"I'll be in touch," he told the mayor.

Those "pictures" were attending school just a few miles away—his children: Jennifer, Allison, and Bobby. What would they think of their dad if it came out he had taken a bribe to get government work?

Weygand went to his car and, using a hand-held tape recorder, recorded to the best of his recollection the exact words that had been exchanged in the mayor's office. If he lost his business he knew he could be forfeiting his children's education, but that wasn't nearly as important as what he'd lose if he accepted the bribe. So he called the state police, they called the FBI, and a few weeks later, Weygand returned to city hall carrying a white envelope filled with $1,250 (in fifty- and hundred-dollar bills). He also brought one thing more…a recording device.

A few weeks later, the mayor asked Weygand about the other $1,750; the architect quickly brought in another envelope. Only this time, when the mayor left his office, FBI agents were waiting to arrest him. A crumpled envelope covered with his fingerprints and $1,750 in marked bills in his front pocket provided all the needed evidence.

So was Weygand a hero? Certainly not to everyone. After the story hit the press, he heard people on radio talk shows calling him a liar. He also received numerous threatening phone calls on his answering machine.

But that didn't matter once he got home.

For there were Jennifer, Allison, and Bobby, all eager to hug him and echo the words, "Daddy, I'm proud of you."

It cost their dad a career and a business to do what was right, but part of being there means we do what's needed regardless of the cost.

It's going to be costly to be there for our children. Costly in terms of time, effort, energy, and lost sleep. But it's well worth every cost.

When our name and eyes and heart are turned toward our children, they'll indeed know that we love them *forever.* And when we choose to be there in the present moment and to make a positive contribution, regardless of the cost, then we'll pave a future without regrets.

And that's a road I'll travel anytime.

A Personal Application Project

To really be there for our children, we first have to know what kind of children they are. We have to know them—their likes and dislikes, their strengths and weaknesses, their idiosyncrasies and unique traits. The following six questions will help you to become a better student of your child:

- "What's one thing Mom (or Dad) could pray about for you today?"
- "If you could be anything, what would you be when you grow up?"
- "What's one thing you really appreciate about your best friend?"
- "If we could go anywhere on vacation, where would we go and what would we do?"
- "What's your favorite thing for us to do as a family that doesn't involve spending any money?"
- "What's one thing Dad (or Mom) could work on that would make you feel even more loved?"

Asking questions to really know your child's hurts and fears, dreams and defeats, can help you to be there for him or her in a powerful way.

Once you've tried out the questions above, here's another list for you of little things that might help you to connect with your children in small ways that can meet a need or make a positive contribution.

Twenty Ways to Be There for Your Children

1. Compliment each of them individually every day. Compliment and encourage your spouse in front of the kids every day also.
2. Give them a hug or other special touch each day.
3. Point out to them that they have a special future and purpose.
4. Set aside time each week to work on a project with the kids. Give them specific tasks that they're in charge of completing.

5. Plan time alone with each child. Use that time to focus on him or her, like a "date night" with Dad or a "guy's time" for Mom.

Be There through Fun Activities

6. Roast marshmallows over the barbecue grill.
7. Make a "fort" with blankets in the kids' rooms and spend time camping with each.
8. Rent a motor home and take the family on weekend trips.
9. Play as many board games as possible before they are teenagers.
10. Coach peewee sports teams. Attend kids' practices and games.
11. Take the kids fishing—almost every child likes the idea of catching a fish.
12. Read books and use puppets with the stories.
13. Blow soap bubbles in the yard on a regular basis.
14. Take hikes and bike rides.

Be There by Sharing in Spiritual Development

15. Take your kids to church and volunteer in their Sunday-school classes.
16. Read one Bible story or chapter together a couple of times per week.
17. Pray with and for your children each morning or night.
18. Serve less fortunate people together—do a missions trip as a family.
19. Attend at least one church service as a family each month.
20. Take time to share with them what God is teaching you during your week.

13 | *Being There for Your Spouse*

Did you know an entire book in the Bible gives specifics on "blooming out" a spouse's life? Now, if that doesn't sound like anything you've read in the Bible lately, just turn past Psalms and Proverbs, and you'll find a rarely preached portrait of a wonderful courtship and marriage. It's a book filled with pictures of what it means to be there for our spouse.

It's called the Song of Solomon, or the Song of Songs. And it starts with a communication tool that can help your loved one feel that, indeed, your name, eyes, and heart are there for him or her...and always will be.

And the Envelope Please...

Do you know why the Bible so often repeats words? You know, like "King of kings" and "Lord of lords"? It's because when an attribute is doubled, it means the thing being described is the very best of all.

In the Song of Songs we find a human love story so special, so instructive, that it tops any other. The winner for Best Picture of a Love Story isn't *Romeo and Juliet* or *Sleepless in Seattle* or even *You've Got Mail* (as if you could really get on-line every time without a single busy signal, as they do in that last movie).

No, the greatest picture of a "love for all seasons" is recorded in the Bible. It really *is* the Song of Songs.

There's no doubt that Solomon's bride blooms right before our eyes. Why? Because of her husband's love. And that's particularly important in her case, because she didn't come from a flowery background.

In the real world of relational bumps and bruises, many people enter marriage with a less-than-ideal picture of who they are and all they can become in Christ. That's not a modern-day phenomenon by a long shot. Listen to the words of Solomon's bride as she confesses a high level of insecurity at the start of their relationship.

> I am black but lovely,
> O daughters of Jerusalem,
> Like the tents of Kedar,
> Like the curtains of Solomon.
> Do not stare at me because I am swarthy,
> For the sun has burned me.
> My mother's sons were angry with me;
> They made me caretaker of the vineyards,
> But I have not taken care of my own vineyard.
> (Song of Solomon 1:5-6)

You can't help but see two things in these first words of Solomon's bride. Number one, she sees potential in herself despite her problems. "I am black *but* lovely," she says. So there's potential there, all right, yet she freely admits that any positives are outweighed by her less-than-perfect past.

First, she's sporting a dark brown tan that didn't come from Sinai Sam's tanning salon. It came from the working-class world where, day after day, she was forced to tend vineyards in the scorching summer sun and wind-swept winters. And while being bronzed and beautiful may win points today, in Old Testament culture, the mere fact that she had soaked up so much color would set her apart from the cultured ladies of the court. Those dainties hid from the sun.

Do you begin to see why this working-class woman who has fallen in love with a king might feel a little insecure? It's not merely that she's the only one around the royal palace with a day job. She's also embarrassed about her past and what it says about her present. As she said, "My mother's sons were angry with me; they made me caretaker of their vineyard, and I have not been able to take care of my own."

Did you notice something significant? She didn't say her "brothers" were the ones making her work on their vineyards; she calls them "my mother's sons." In other words, her father is dead or gone, and it's angry stepbrothers or half brothers who demand all her efforts go into *their* vineyards.

Why was that so shameful to her?

Because by spending all her time working on a harvest for *them*, she had no harvest of her own, meaning no dowry for a marriage (a terrible thing in those days).

Is the picture of how she viewed herself getting even clearer? She's a woman who knows she's lovely, yet is from a far-less-than-perfect family. Add to that her financial insecurity, and it's no wonder she feels she has nothing to offer.

And so she stands in front of her fiancé and stammers, "Do not look at me!"

The marks of the sun and a painful past have darkened any feelings of worth or acceptance. Yet that's not the end of the story, but only the beginning.

A Real-Life *My Fair Lady*

Turn just a few pages in the Song of Solomon and you can see what being there for someone does for their self-image. Solomon's bride goes from saying, "Don't look at me!" to saying this:

> I am the rose of Sharon, the lily of the valleys. (2:1)

Now *that's* a paradigm shift. From words of insecurity to a cry of confidence and joy. But why did it happen? And more important, *how* could such a massive switch in perspective take place?

In the musical *My Fair Lady*, the change agent that transformed Eliza Doolittle into someone who carried herself like a duchess, was none other than...*words*.

Incredible, isn't it? A few syllables, whether spoken or written, had the ability to turn an uncouth flower girl into a person of substance and character. This woman, who at the beginning wouldn't hold her head up and look directly at the professor, changed into a confident, radiant beauty with her head lifted high in any company.

But that's just for movies and screenplays...right?

Wrong.

In God's Word, words are shown to be a powerful way of being there for a real person. The right ones, spoken in the right way and at the right time, have the power to "bloom out a life," to help a man or woman get a new picture of their personhood and potential.

Ready to see just what this wise husband did to add sand and mortar to his bride's sagging self-confidence? Here are the very words:

> To me, my darling, you are like my mare among the chariots of Pharaoh. (1:9)

You mean, that's it? All I have to do is to compare my mate to a smelly animal? The next time he or she walks into the room, I'm supposed to put down this book and say, "Honey, you know those Clydesdales we saw at the last parade? Remember? The really big horses with all that white drool all over them, pulling that huge wagon? Well, honey, I want you to know that, to me, you're just like a big old horse...only you don't sweat as much."

Touching, no?

I know that saying to your spouse "You're like a mare" doesn't seem significant enough to change a person's self-perspective. In fact, for most husbands today, calling your spouse a horse would indeed be an eye-opening experience...and about two weeks later your *other* eye would open.

Yet that's because we don't get the picture Solomon uses.

But she did.

That's because the king used a picture unfamiliar to us, but one that people of her day carried in their minds and memory banks.

But of a horse?

Did you know the standard railroad gauge today is 4 feet 8.5 inches? That was the width of the ruts left in old English roads by a two-horse war chariot.

Did you notice I said, *"two-horse chariot"*?

The standard war chariot of the day carried two men, not one, and was pulled by two stallions each, not one.

But not Pharaoh's chariot. His broke the mold. When Solomon says to his insecure bride, "To me, my darling, you are like my mare among the chariots of Pharaoh," he's pointing out a fact known to most everyone in that day. Pharaoh picked a mare to guide his chariot, not a stallion. And his chariot was built for one horse, not two—unique from all others.

In other words, Solomon is saying to her, "Darling, you know how Pharaoh could have chosen any mare in all the land to pull his personal chariot? In the same way, I could have chosen any woman in the land—*and I chose you.*"

The first thing we must keep in mind in order to be there for our spouse is the importance of our words. Our words shape and encourage, or at their worst, slam and demean. Words have the power to change a person's perspective. They don't merely affect an Eliza Doolittle or an insecure bride in the Bible. They can make a huge difference in your own marriage as well.

They Won't Buy It If They Can't See It

"I'm not buying that," someone might say. "You're saying that one major way to be there for my spouse is to use *words* to give her (or him) a different picture of herself (or himself)? And that some type of *picture* can make a real difference in how they perceive themselves? *Prove it to me!*"

Fair enough. First, let's look at what happens in your spouse's brain when you give him or her a picture that reflects a positive character trait you want her or him to own. Whether we're trying to get someone to buy a product or buy into a new way of looking at themselves, it takes words to make the sale.

Roy Williams, the marketing expert known as "The Wizard of Ads," in his thought-provoking *Monday Morning Memo* makes and backs up the following statement: "A customer can do nothing that he has not 'seen himself do' in his mind."

What does that mean?

"Mental imagery or 'seeing things' in the mind, takes place on the brain's Visuospatial Sketchpad, one of the three functions of working memory," Williams says. (Stay with me on this—it gets a little complicated regarding brain function, but the end result will amaze you.) He continues:

Common sense would tell us that the Visuospatial Sketch-pad would be contained in the *Visual Association Area* at the back of the skull, but then common sense would be wrong. All three functions of working memory, including the Visuospatial Sketchpad, are located in the Dorolateral Prefrontal Association Area (DLPFC).

Okay. And the point?

The DLPFC is a bridge between the *Auditory Association Area* (near the ear) and the *Prefrontal Cortex* (the area behind the forehead, which is the decision making center for planning, emotion, and judgment). It is on this DLPFC Bridge that your customer "sees" himself taking action. When your customer sees things in his imagination, like the sun rising over the ocean, *the part of the brain he's using is not connected to his eye, but is connected to his ear!*

Do you see what he's driving at? If not, listen once more:

Words, when spoken well or artfully, can cause your customer to see things in his mind; things that you want him to actually experience.[1]

Effective, well-chosen words help people "see themselves" doing something different—and they can help someone *become* something different as well. The words in God's Word help us see all our potential and purpose; they are "a lamp to our feet and a light to our path." It was words that changed Eliza Doolittle into a duchess. Why? Because as she began to use words fit for a queen, she saw in those words the new, more valuable person she was becoming.

No wonder that, over forty times in the eight short chapters of this Old Testament book, Solomon gives a new picture to his bride. As she heard these positive words and understood that she was chosen, special, and deeply loved, her internal picture of herself changed. Gone was the snapshot of an insecure flower girl who wanted her prince to look away. In its place appeared someone who felt so loved and secure that she felt like putting herself on display. She cries in happiness, "I am the rose of sharon, the lily of the valleys!"

And then something remarkable happens. No longer is it only the husband who chooses to be there in using words to build up his wife. Suddenly she gets into the act as well.

Some thirty times in these eight chapters she builds up *his* life with her words of praise. For example, look at this picture she gives him:

> Like an apple tree among the trees of the forest, so is my
> beloved among the young men. (2:3)

Now, don't even think she just called her husband a "fruit."

She's not criticizing him; she's giving him a mental snapshot of the way she pictures him. He's an apple tree in the midst of a forest.

Have you ever been lost in a pine forest?

Take it from someone who's been lost in the woods way too often (just ask my children), all pine trees begin to look alike after a while. But how refreshing it is to walk into a clearing and suddenly see an exception: a tree that not only draws nutrients from the ground, but gives back nutritious and tasty fruit to the person who sits under its shade.

That's how his bride pictures Solomon.

As a care*giver*—not just a taker.

And that's another crucial aspect of what it means to be there for our spouses. We must become givers, not merely takers.

It's About Producing Apples, Not Just Picking Them

George Bernard Shaw, the Irish author and raconteur who wrote *Pygmalion* (the inspiration for *My Fair Lady*), once said, "We have no more right to consume happiness without producing it than to consume wealth without producing it."

In his early days, Solomon wasn't someone who just took from life and from his marital relationship. He was a giver of nutrition, an apple tree among all those pine trees.

Let me say it as plainly as did George Bernard Shaw.

It requires more than takers to create a be-there marriage.

Just ask Alice. She can tell you.

Alice happened to be cleaning my teeth the other day when I went in for my semiannual checkup. While I've had the same dentist for years, this was the first time Alice had cleaned my teeth. She was professional and courteous…and brokenhearted.

When she found out I was a counselor, she quickly described her ten-year marriage to a taker.

Alice remarried just a year after the death of her first husband, who had died from cancer. Her second husband had never been married, even though he was in his forties. During their courtship, it looked as if this would be a relationship that could turn ashes of sorrow into beauty.

It turned out to be ten more years of ashes.

That's because Alice was married to a "pine tree" and not to an "apple tree." He took, but he didn't give back the nutrition she needed. Even though they were married in a church (and even met there), he never went with her to church after the wedding. To help her "keep her identity" (his words), he refused to give her his last name, urging her instead to keep her former name on the marriage certificate and mailing address. That should have been a red flag.

For ten years, he lived as a married single. Protective of his time, demanding of his "rights," jealous of his hobbies, unwilling to get a joint checking account or to share any financial information—he took and took and took some more. What's more, he refused to visit, speak on the phone with, or buy presents for any of Alice's three children (from her first marriage) or her seven grandchildren. Which is why Alice became a hygienist; she wanted to have her own money to visit her kids or send them a present.

Ten years of living with a taker. Of living with someone who had refused to be there for her needs, her family, her dreams. The man was a pine tree, not an apple tree.

With such a history, it didn't surprise me to hear recently that he'd moved on and found someone younger to move in with. Finally, he did serve his wife—not with the nourishing fruit of a be-there attitude, but with divorce papers.

Now, to be fair, it's not only husbands who focus solely on themselves. There are many wives who do all the taking and no giving. These women, too, are pine trees rather than apple trees. For whatever reason, they refuse to be there for their husband with positive words or affection or friendship or financial responsibility or faithfulness…and so the marriage goes south.

But marriages don't have to go in that direction.

We really can be there for our spouses. It is our great privilege to help them, through our words, picture all they can become in Christ. God calls us to become givers in a land full of takers.

And we do so by paying attention to the four benchmarks we've already identified.

14 | *More Help for a Be-There Marriage*

Has there ever been a more heartwarming overnight sensation in professional sports than Kurt Warner, the rags-to-riches quarterback of the St. Louis Rams?

Kurt's remarkable story began with a college scholarship to Northern Iowa, where he sat on the bench for four years before leading his team to the NCAA Division I-AA semifinals as a fifth-year senior. The Green Bay Packers were impressed enough to give him a contract, but he soon washed out of the NFL. A discouraged Kurt returned to Cedar Falls, Iowa, worked out at the college during the day, and for $5.50 an hour, stocked shelves each night at the Hy-Vee grocery store.

But his days of handling groceries were numbered. After short stints in the Arena Football League and NFL Europe, Kurt barely made the roster of the Rams as a third-string backup. But when the team's starter went down in a preseason game with a serious knee injury, Kurt got his chance—and the rest, as they say, is history. He led his team to the NFC championship and then to victory in Super Bowl XXXIV, all the while leading the league in about a dozen statistical categories.

But that's not why many consider him a hero, as an article in *USA Today* makes clear.

In the article headlined "Rams' Warner Armed with Love,"[1] reporter Jill Lieber focuses on the stable, loving home life Kurt has created for his family. He met his wife, Brenda, in 1992 when he was a twenty-year-old junior in college and she was a twenty-four-year-old recent divorcée with two children—an infant and a two-year-old son with serious medical problems. The couple met at a barn dance and hit it off immediately, but the night Brenda told Kurt about her situation, she was sure he'd disappear.

Instead Kurt showed up at her house the next morning to meet the kids, a rose in hand. It didn't matter to Kurt that Brenda's son, Zachary, had suffered some brain damage in a household accident that also left him nearly blind. "He fell in love with the kids before he fell in love with me," Brenda says. These days, Zachary often falls asleep on his adopted father's chest.

Kurt is a be-there kind of dad and husband who puts his family first. He gushes over his wife and often says things like, "The way she has handled challenges has made me love her more. She has shown me the best way to respond when you go through struggles. She's a tremendous inspiration to me."

And you don't have to guess what his kids think about him. When the Warners returned home after the Rams won the NFC title game, they immediately hugged all their kids and got ready to sit down to eat. But before they said grace, the children surprised their dad with a huge card, decorated in the Rams' team colors, festooned with hearts and topped by a single line written in a childlike scribble: "You're as Great a Dad as You Are a Quarterback."

How's that for winning two championships in a single day?

Kurt Warner is a be-there kind of man. He chooses to connect with his wife and kids, is "all there" in the present moment, sees a need and makes a positive contribution, and does it regardless of the cost.

May his tribe increase!

Open Your Eyes

Did you know that from the moment you first see your spouse in the morning (even with bed-head hair or wrinkled jammies), you can *choose* to be there for him or her—just by opening your eyes?

The book of Proverbs tells us, "Bright eyes gladden the heart" (15:30). That means that just by opening your eyes—by really choosing to look at your spouse with more interest than you do the morning paper or a television commercial—you can bring great joy into the world.

We make married hearts glad by opening our eyes to see what *they* need to accomplish today...and by praying and helping them to reach that goal or finish that chore. We bring joy into their world by opening our eyes to what *they* want to say to us, instead of putting off discussion for another time. We give them happiness by making the choice to "open our eyes" to what's not quite right in our relationship...and filling in those be-there benchmarks to actively, positively make things better.

In this day and age, if you don't set your schedule to connect, someone or something will set it for you. How much better for you to be the one doing the setting. *Choose* to connect with your mate.

Focus on Today

My precious wife, Cindy, and I both came from homes far from the "street of dreams." Mine was a single-parent home, and Cindy's was an alcoholic home. Both of us have had to make a serious commitment to be there in the present moment for each other—because we represent two polar opposites.

I'm the one who, like the disciples, gets caught up arguing over "all the good that's bound to come" and who misses the good in *today*. I find

125

myself always looking ahead. At the next vacation instead of the one we're on. Looking forward to the next project instead of taking the time right now to rest and reconnect. I'm good at brainstorming sessions that bring even more potential opportunities for future ministry…without factoring in how those future dreams impact what I'm called to do today.

But you don't connect with your spouse in the present if your focus is always on the future. The days and weeks can speed by before you realize, too late, that you haven't really looked, really listened, really pictured something positive for your spouse. Remember, we can look, listen, and draw positive pictures for our spouses only in the present.

Are you so focused on the future that it's keeping you from being there today? Would your spouse answer that question in the same way you do?

Or are you more like Cindy and sometimes get stuck in the past?

Cindy would be the first to declare that things have changed dramatically and positively in her family. Her father no longer drinks. Several family members have become Christians, and family gatherings are radically improved from what she recalls as a child. But still, some of those negative childhood memories can lure her to focus on what happened instead of what's here today, to camp in the past instead of the present.

Something about trauma projects the pictures in our memory at a slow speed. It can lock negative images into our brain and keep replaying them again and again and again. If that describes you, I wrote a whole book just for you called *Pictures the Heart Remembers*. If you need to deal with past hurts, I unashamedly urge you to get a copy of this book.

My wife has done a wonderful job of "moving on." She's taken the lead in asking forgiveness and forgiving, in putting pieces back together and staying positive and committed. But even today there are times when her focus drifts to the past and locks on to one of those negative pictures. When that happens, it can leave less of her heart and mind to connect with me or the girls.

Cindy knows that when she's tired or stressed or hurting, she tends to look back to the past. It's her default setting. But she also knows there's another, more meaningful option. She can reframe those negative pictures and put herself and her loved ones in the present.

And so can you.

Give a Clear Target

Did you know that it isn't the big things that build a marriage but the little ones?

Christians will notice immediately that there is a biblical precedent for that. The one who gets rewarded with much is the one who's "faithful in a little," according to Jesus.

With that in mind, let me ask you to do something that can make a positive difference in your marriage, even though it may come as a blow to your pride.

Here it is: *Give your spouse a clear target to shoot for when it comes to meeting your needs.*

It's important not to keep your spouse guessing at what specific needs or contributions he or she can make. It's not too much to write down those "inner lines" that you feel would enrich your marriage—and put them in a place where your spouse can see them.

"No way!" I hear someone objecting. "I'm not going to tell him *again* what he needs to do to make me feel loved or special. He should just *know!*"

And then there's the follow-up.

"Besides, if she *did* do something on my list, then it would just be because *you* said to write it down, not because she *felt* like doing it."

Listen, friend, neither argument holds water. They're both as full of holes as a blue-ribbon Swiss cheese round at the Wisconsin State Fair. Every year that I spend as a trained counselor only strengthens my judgment on this issue. The truth is, *the average person needs to be shown the target.*

We need to write down the specifics of what, for each of us, constitute love and caring. We need to see, in black and white, a clear picture of what progress and closeness look like in our eyes.

So do me a favor. If your spouse does something on your "list"—even if it's something *you* wrote down and he or she didn't intuitively know it— give your honey full credit for the deposit into your account. You'll be glad you did. And so will your mate.

Keep the Demon in His Place

Good marriages don't just happen. There is no such thing as finding the "right" one and then sitting back as all the pieces fall naturally into place. Even those who do manage to find the perfect mate discover pretty early on that building a warm, caring, satisfying marriage takes a lot of work. There's a cost to be paid, and often it's a high one.

On the other hand, the return on investment can be phenomenal.

Here's what Norman Vincent Peale said about the cost of a good marriage, as well as its unique rewards:

> I can speak about marriage with conviction because, having been married for over 40 years to the same wonderful woman, I can testify that there is nothing else like the closeness, the mutual support, the deep affection and companionship that grow between a man and a woman who have fought the battles of life together for years and

years. Pleasures are brighter because you share them. Problems are lighter because you face them together. There's no describing these things, really; you have to experience them to know them. And the only way to experience them is to set one shining goal in marriage, *permanence,* and stick to it no matter what adversities you may encounter along the way.

Peale, best known for his book *The Power of Positive Thinking,* didn't simply look the other way when marital troubles came calling. He knew the costs involved in a be-there kind of marriage. But he also knew the rewards. Read on for more of his insight:

> Difficult? Of course it's difficult! Each of us has within us a little demon called ego that never ceases resisting the compromises and disciplines and acts of selflessness and control that must become not just occasional, but habitual, if a marriage is to become a really good one.
> But when that demon is put and kept in its place, the rewards are beyond all reckoning.[2]

If you want to be there for your wife or husband, you must realize that such commitment *costs.* There are no bargain-basement marriages, except in basements. And you don't get much light there.

A Personal Application Project

To help you be there for your spouse, I'd like you to pick up a pen or pencil and write down three things *right now* that your spouse could do for you. By that, I mean small, specific, positive, caring things—that when done would say to you, "I'm loved and very special."

Small things like, "Call me from work." Or, "Give the kids a bath for me." Or, "Give me a five-minute backrub…no strings attached." And on your list of three things, *no dirty positives*. In other words, no writing verbal or written hooks like, "Please take out the trash *for the first time in your life.*"

So, get ready…get set…go! Write down your three small, specific, positive ways your spouse can hit the target dead center to communicate that he or she really cares.

1.

2.

3.

Just in case you need some help in priming the pump, consider the following twenty ways to be there for your spouse that you could add in the days and weeks to come.

1. Keep mistletoe hung in your home year-round.
2. Warm your spouse's towel in the dryer before he or she gets out of the shower or bath.
3. Celebrate the anniversary of when you first met.
4. Celebrate your spouse's half-birthday each year.
5. Drape a giant banner in front of your house to celebrate his or her return from a trip.
6. Take your wife to dinner during the Super Bowl (tape it and watch it later).
7. Write letters that say how much you believe in each other and frame them.
8. Set aside twenty minutes each day, right after you get home from work, to ask about each other's day.

9. Write encouraging messages on the eggs in the refrigerator for your spouse to find.

10. Leave love notes in his or her favorite books or magazines.

11. Take turns making breakfast for each other.

12. Set a standing date for one or two meals each week. Share waffles every Thursday morning and a lunch date away from work on the same day every week.

13. Kiss his or her palm and close his or her fingers into a fist and say, "Save this."

14. Rent his or her favorite movies—even on weeknights.

15. Window-shop together.

16. Write a letter and send it to his or her workplace.

17. Make frequent phone calls during each day to check in.

18. Exercise together—walking, jogging, weightlifting, basketball, etc.

19. Thank each other repeatedly for the "small things" you do for one another (folding laundry, cooking meals, cleaning, doing yard work, going to work each day, bathing the kids, giving compliments, etc.).

20. Set up a secret way to say "I love you" in public—like squeezing each other's hand three times.

(I know I said "twenty," but here are ten more for good measure—and an even better relationship.)

21. Open doors for your wife.

22. Compliment your husband in public.

23. Order an unexpected late-night pizza.

24. Say, "I'm sorry, It's my fault."

25. Match what you want to do with what you actually do.

26. Show affection even when you don't feel affectionate.

27. Make time each day to tell your spouse what you appreciate about him or her.
28. Always share the duties of child-rearing.
29. Say "I love you" as often as your spouse can stand it.
30. On your spouse's birthday, write a thank-you note to his or her parents.

15 | *Being There for Your Friends*

What is a true friend?

The dictionary can get you only so far. It offers bland definitions like "a person attached to another by feelings of affection or personal regard" or "one joined to another in mutual benevolence and intimacy."

Bleah.

Can you imagine saying to your best friend, "Ryan, I am so glad that we are attached to one another by feelings of affection or personal regard," or, "Mary, we are so fortunate to be joined to one another in mutual benevolence and intimacy"? I can't either.

So what is a true friend? What is a best friend?

I don't think I'd be too wide of the mark to suggest that best friends are those who embody all four of the main qualities we've looked at in this book. Let's start with the first, having our *name* be there for our friends.

Friends and Brothers

Every time my twin brother, Jeff, and I went through the lunch line in grade school, we were glad our name was Hamilton.

Confused? Don't be. Although legally our name remained Trent, while we stood in line for lunch we were blood brothers of our best friend, Eric Hamilton—who just happened to have a secret admirer in the cafeteria.

His mother.

Do you remember Tater Tots? Those incredibly good, little hash-brown-type nuggets that you could never get enough of? We got more Tater Tots than we could handle. That's because every time we went through the lunch line with our best friend—Hambone, as everyone called him—Mrs. Hamilton would ladle out to us a double portion of anything. Including those prized, delicious Tater Tots.

Why? Because our friend bestowed his name on us. We were honorary Hamilton boys.

So many people I talk to feel as if their best friend's family has "adopted" them. Cared for them. Taken care of them. And that's the way it should be.

If my friend carries my name, and if his name is on us, that delightful fact should show up in the way we meet each other's needs, in how we gladly and instinctively reach out a helping hand, or in how we greet our friend with a flurry of hugs or handshakes.

Or if your name is Hamilton, in an extra ladle of Tater Tots.

Rendezvous at Rocky Point

If I squint my eyes and take a long look back in my memory, I can see miles of bright, sunny beaches. Waves splash on jagged rocks, creating small tidal pools containing enough sea life to keep three young boys occupied for hours.

I'll never forget the afternoon my mother called us boys outside to see what had followed her home. It was a Friday afternoon, right after lunch, and Mom had come home early from work…her car trailed by a tiny aluminum trailer hitched to our Falcon. It was called a teardrop trailer because of its unique shape, like a teardrop laid on its side. It was obviously well used and couldn't have stretched over nine feet long from hitch to taillight.

When you opened its single side door, you saw a full-size mattress that covered the entire floor of the trailer. That mattress was just big enough for the four of us to huddle together in our sleeping bags. And though our new home-on-wheels wasn't tall enough for even us boys to stand up inside, there was plenty of room to cram in all the essentials for a camping trip: sodas and armies of toy soldiers, mountains of snacks, softball gloves, footballs, swimsuits…and even some camping equipment.

For the first time ever in our family, we were going camping. And not just anywhere—we were going camping on the beach *in Mexico.*

You have to understand what a stretch that was for my mother. She had grown up in affluence in the home of her uncle, who was a physician in Indiana. She'd never been camping as a child. She'd never been to Mexico. She'd never pulled a trailer. But she knew that three active boys, ages six and six and eight, needed some outdoor education—so we packed up the teardrop and headed south from Phoenix.

It was 1958, long before any single-parent support groups had organized to help pull together a campout. So, all alone, Mom bravely made the six-hour trek toward Tucson and then to the Mexican border. From there, it was another three hours to a place we gringos called Rocky Point (and the Mexicans called Pointe Penasco).

We boys came to call it Kid Heaven.

But it wasn't heaven that first night.

Mom had never used a Coleman heater, lantern, or stove (all new and right out of the box), and after the long drive it was pitch black by the time we finally reached the beach. Still, we took turns for what seemed like hours trying to get anything besides those white mantles to burn for more than a few seconds. We finally gave up and ate cold cereal for dinner by the dim glow of a fading flashlight (our only light source).

Mom had parked the car and trailer close to the beach. When we woke up, a cold wind was howling off the ocean. Strong gusts rocked our little trailer, and the wind-driven sand blasted our faces when we dared to peek outside.

Huddled together—cold, hungry, discouraged, and miserable—we waited sullenly for the first one to toss in the towel so we could all head home in defeat.

And that's when God gave us an entire caravan of trucks and trailers that drove right into our camping area—or at least God loaned them to us.

Almost a dozen vehicles of all shapes and sizes, many with *real* trailers, pulled into the wide public camping area we had picked. Soon dads and moms and kids of all ages were piling out of cars, setting up tents, and even getting stoves lit for hot cocoa and coffee. During this whole time, like cans of corn stacked one on top of each other, four heads peeked out of our trailer door and watched enviously as these camping pros laughed and warmed themselves beside a roaring campfire.

And then something special happened.

Someone in this group put on God's kind of 3-D glasses.

As we cracked open the door to our trailer so we could see the new visitors, a sudden gust of wind flung the door wide open. My older brother, Joe, had to scramble outside to push it nearly closed so we could peek out again. But once the door flew open, we noticed a middle-aged man with a leathery tan had begun to watch us.

He was bent down next to the fire, warming himself and drinking a cup of coffee, studying us. Then he straightened up and walked over to our trailer.

The smile lighting up his face had stayed bright and sunny through raising two now-grown sons of his own. And he earned the weather-beaten look as a deck officer on a destroyer during World War II.

We didn't know it, but we had parked our trailer at the favorite camp-site of a very unofficial camping club from Phoenix. This jolly group of businesspeople took off their ties, gathered their families, and drove down to Rocky Point once or twice a month. And as it turned out, their unofficial leader was now standing right in front of three wide-eyed boys and their nearly frozen mother.

"Y'all want to come over and have some hot chocolate?" he asked in his soft voice, with the "y'all" a fixed part of his South Carolina accent.

One look at Mom, who nodded her head, and we were out the door in a flash, huddling by the fire. Soon we were thawed, laughing, and meet-ing kids our own age. And Mom was enjoying a cup of coffee, getting a lesson on lighting our Coleman stove, and thanking the Lord she was no longer alone in a strange country where she didn't speak the language or know the ropes of camping.

That afternoon the clouds blew past, the sun appeared, and we scur-ried up and down the beach a hundred times. By Sunday we had all shared meals and campfires and lighting firecrackers…and one more thing.

Friendship.

When the weekend came to a close, this new group of friends asked my mom if we'd like to become an official family in the Cholla Bay Wad-ing, Ruckus, and Burnt Food Society. Brushing back tears and joining the delirious echo of three young boys, Mom said, "Yes."

That's the difference a friend can make when he cocks his eye toward us and really looks. And what the eye of a friend sees, the heart of a friend moves to warm and encourage.

That's what it means to be there.

For the next five years, we spent dozens of weekends pitching our tent with these friends, sharing the drive, watching our gear when we were at the beach, and giving us a warm spot at their fire if we couldn't get ours started. These were friends who knew how to be there for us with their name and eyes and heart. And it all started with a few words softly spoken by a man who reached out a hand of friendship—and three mugs of hot chocolate and a cup of coffee.

We came to find out that "Uncle Don" got his 3-D glasses by floating around on a lifeboat after his ship had been sunk in the Solomon Islands. In those lonely and terrifying hours on the raft he'd given his life to Christ. He knew well the look of fear and of being cold and of someone needing a friend to be there for them. So with his 3-D glasses given to him by his Friend, Jesus, he saw what others didn't when they looked past a broken-down teardrop trailer. God lit up our need, and with his Father's eyes, Don saw our plight and came to our rescue.

That's a true friend. Don defined for us the meaning of *friend*, even if he never used the words *mutual benevolence* or *personal regard*.

Brothers and Friends

True friends don't have to sport a last name different from your own. Family can become be-there friends as well.

I'll never forget the time in high school I picked up the phone at the same time that my twin brother, Jeff, did. Without his knowledge, I was on the line and heard Jeff talking to someone who was asking him—and not me—to a sleepover party.

I'll confess to a few moments of anxiety. I didn't know for sure what Jeff would say. Would he leave me out of the deal? Would he forget about his brother for the sake of a good time?

Jeff didn't miss a beat. He stated matter-of-factly, "If I'm going, John's going. If he's not, I'm not."

You couldn't have doused the grin on my face with a ten-thousand-gallon high-pressure hose.

That's how my mom raised us. To be there as best friends, forever, as well as brothers. Best friends stick together always, and Jeff was my best friend in the whole world.

The same goes for my awesome big brother, Joe. If it's three in the morning, and your car's broken down in Yuma, he'll drive the five hours to be there when you call. Joe has *always* been there for me. Protecting me. Caring for me. We were in the room together when Mom died, one son on one side holding her hand, one on the other. I couldn't have made it without him.

We all need friends we can cry with and who can hurt with us. And beyond my brothers, I'm glad I have several others whose hearts are there for me whenever I call.

Always.

Forever.

It's *that* kind of buddy who will help you to understand "what is a friend?"—and drive the comforting knowledge far deeper into your brain than a stack of frozen dictionary definitions piled three miles high.

A Personal Application Project

How about you? Do you have this type of be-there friends? If not, then perhaps it's time to realize that it's the small things that can help build strong connections—small things like the list of be-there friendship traits below. It's a short list, but it's ready for you to add lots of items that can mark your friendships as genuine treasures.

Marks of a Be-There Friend

A be-there friend is someone who...

- will laugh at your joke as if he never heard that one before.
- will automatically volunteer to watch your kids when you have an important appointment.
- begins conversations by asking questions about how you're doing.
- takes the risk to tell you when you're off track, but stays with you through the healing process. ("A friend loves at all times"— Proverbs 17:17.)
- loans you his pickup and helps you move across town.
- after borrowing your truck, returns your vehicle with a full gas tank and doesn't tell you he filled it up.
- thanks you for pointing out a mistake, shortcoming, or sin. ("Oil and perfume make the heart glad, so a man's counsel is sweet to his friend"—Proverbs 27:9.)
- admits he was wrong and accepts your counsel. ("A good man loves justice"—Proverbs 21:15, TLB.)
- automatically looks for the best in you.
- defends you when you are not around to do it yourself.
- prays with you over the phone instead of just saying, "I'll pray for you."
- remembers your last conversation and the next time you talk asks how things turned out.
- invites you over for dinner when your spouse is out of town
- compliments and encourages you, out of the blue.
- shares appropriate touches (hugs, handshakes, nudges, etc.).
- tells you that you can do anything if you set your mind to it (validates your competence).
- stays up with you at the hospital during a family emergency.
- helps you landscape your yard in the middle of the summer.

- treats your children as if they were his or hers.
- won't hesitate to shed tears with you and for you.
- doesn't say, "If there's anything you need, just call," but *does* something on your behalf when he sees the need.

What would you add? What is a be-there friend in your personal dictionary? How do you strive to be there for your friends? Make another list and, if possible, share it with your best friend.

16 | *Being There for the World Around You*

I'm sure some long-forgotten planning committee or board of trustees came up with the name, Children's Hospital of Pittsburgh. But that wonderful institution really should change its stationery as well as the sign out front. That's because a different name is "written" all over that hospital and its dedicated staff—and especially on the very sick children who come there with such serious needs.

Just stroll down the hospital hallways and it's obvious that it really should be called *Albert Lexie Hospital.*

Shoeshining Albert

"Hey! It's Mr. Celebrity!" a smiling nurse calls out as Albert Lexie hurries down a hospital hallway. But Albert doesn't have time to do anything but give her a quick wave. You see, he's on a mission from God. Not the kind of senseless Blues Brothers mission that works only for a few cheap laughs. This mission is serious business because Albert is on his way to serve sick kids…kids who gladly wear his name.[1]

You couldn't imagine anyone less likely to reach celebrity status. Albert's father left when he was only an infant. His mother had to work full-time while raising Albert and his two sisters. He also would grow up with mental disabilities that limited his ability to learn…but not to love.

Albert was in high school when God gave him a tool that eventually allowed him to help hundreds of lives. His shop teacher assigned everyone in class the task of making a shoeshine kit. While most kids probably tossed their creations in a closet after getting their grade or used the wood for a skateboard or display case or something "more important," Albert took his kit home to use…and he never looked back.

Shoeshining would become Albert's specialty—and one day, his calling.

Albert started his own shoeshine shop after he finished school. He threw himself into the business. Soon he was making enough to live on his own and to fill his little apartment with Christian music cassettes and even a small TV. It was while he was watching a local religious channel that God gave him his mission.

That day, Albert saw a spokesperson for the Children's Hospital in Pittsburgh asking for donations. The speaker patiently explained how the hospital needed money for critically ill children whose parents couldn't afford medical care.

That's all Albert needed to hear. He didn't change the channel to something less convicting; instead he changed into his best clothes, went to his local bank, withdrew the entire $750 he had in savings, and took it to the hospital to help those sick children.

That was nearly twenty years ago.

Today, five days a week, Albert still shines shoes. Each Monday, Wednesday, and Friday he travels to the towns of Charleroi, Monessen, Donora, and Monongahela near Pittsburgh, where he regularly shines more than a hundred pairs of shoes. That's how he makes his living. Then on Tuesdays and Thursdays he gets up (while it's still pitch black outside) to take one bus that can take him to another bus that takes him at last to his shoeshine stand at Children's Hospital.

Albert's going rate for a shine is two dollars. That puts bread and milk on his table. But anything *over* that two dollars goes directly into Albert's Fund, an account kept by the hospital. It's carefully recorded each day, and once a year, in February (the anniversary of the month he first came to the hospital), Albert donates all his tips to the hospital's Free Care Fund. Every cent Albert raises over two dollars goes to very sick children without healthcare, living within a hundred miles of the hospital, so they can receive the medical treatment they so desperately need.

Albert's Sweeties

That might sound like a cute, or perhaps even touching, story, but there's more to it than someone just doing good deeds. When asked why he visits the sickest of children on his days off and why he donates all his tips to them, he replies that it's because these aren't just *any* children in the hospital.

"They're my sweeties," Albert explains. "They're Albert's sweeties."

In other words, they're children who carry his name.

Legally, of course, the names on their birth certificates still read Smith or Jones or Martinez or Maxwell or Brown. But as far as Albert is concerned, each sick child who comes through the hospital door carries his name as well. They're his sweeties.

Albert is living proof that being there for someone else is a powerful way to gain purpose and meaning in life, to find strength you never knew for a task that's bigger than you could imagine.

Albert has gained all that and more in his eagerness to be there for these children, in putting his name on them. He's not a physician or a pharmacist or a scientist who can find a cure for what ails them physically. But he's outstanding at shining shoes and making sacrifices. So shoe by shoe, tip by tip, year by year since 1981, Albert has done a great deal more than his share.

In fact, he has personally donated more than $44,000 to the hospital to help his precious, hurting kids…*every cent earned one shoe at a time.*

Today, Albert is a full-fledged celebrity. He's been written up in the local papers and in *Reader's Digest,* and he even won a prestigious Jefferson Award for Public Service. But for the sixteen years before Albert received a single write-up, award, or public service medal, and every day since, his life has been about being a servant, not a celebrity.

Albert isn't about seeking headlines; he just wants to serve, comfort, and encourage sick children. His name—his *essence,* all he is—is there for his sweeties who so urgently need his love and prayers and help. If the children and staff at the hospital could vote on the zoning committee, no doubt they'd change the name out front to Albert's Kids Hospital.

But where does Albert Lexie get his dedication and stamina to get up on freezing cold winter mornings to catch a 4:30 bus in order to catch the 6 A.M. bus to ride two hours to end up at the hospital—just so he can get down on his knees and shine shoes all day?

Not surprisingly, he gets it from the same source of strength my mom drew upon during those tough days as a rheumatoid arthritic, when she determined to be there for the three boys who carried her name. He gets it from the same source that so many others throughout history have tapped to find the strength to be there for *their* sweeties. All of them have looked to the One who awakened Solomon so long ago and said, "My name will be there forever."

At the ceremony for the Jefferson Award he received, Albert told a packed audience all about his source of strength:

"I want to thank all of you and thank the Lord," he said. "Without him, this wouldn't have happened. The Lord gets all the credit for what I do."

It's his faith that has empowered Albert to get up day after day these last twenty years and put his name on these children. It's the cross of Christ that motivates him to get on his knees day after day and shine someone else's life, one shoe at a time.

And it's the cross of Christ that calls you and me to do the same for the sick and downtrodden in our own communities.

When Congressman John Kasik of Michigan met Albert to thank him for his wonderful example of courage and commitment, the legislator found himself the one being served and encouraged. You see, as Albert was shining the congressman's shoes, he asked him, "Do you mind if I sing you a song?"

Still on his knees, Albert began to sing,

> On a hill far away stood an old rugged cross,
> The emblem of suffering and shame;
> And I love that old cross where the dearest and best
> For a world of lost sinners was slain.
> So I'll cherish the old rugged cross,
> 'Til my trophies at last I lay down;
> I will cling to the old rugged cross,
> And exchange it someday for a crown.

By the time he had finished singing, Kasik writes, "The hallway of the hospital was crowded with doctors and nurses who had stepped outside their doors to listen and applaud."

Can you imagine?

Medical specialists stopping to listen to and applaud a shoeshine man?

I can see it.

Whatever a person's day job, the very best kind of people are shoeshine people. They inspire me to pray, "Lord, help us to be better shoeshine people. Help us to make the commitment to be there for our own sweeties, and to put our whole name into loving them. Amen."

Touched by a Guard-Gun Angel

It was almost Christmas Day and Lieutenant John McCain was being given yet another "attitude adjustment session" by his sadistic Vietnamese captors. He had been caught talking with another prisoner again and was being beaten for his offense.

In his touching book, *Faith of My Fathers,* McCain tells how one interrogator in particular delighted in brutality.[2] He would approach McCain each day and demand that he bow before him. If McCain refused, or even if he did bow, the guard would smash his fist into the side of his head, knocking him to the ground. In McCain's words, "Those encounters were not episodic. They occurred every morning for nearly two years."

Try to imagine being trapped in that kind of bleak setting. A place of cruelty and torture and death…and now Christmas Day just hours away. Far from friends and family, you're beaten unconscious and tied to a chair lying on its side on the filthy floor. That's what happened after one brutal session in which McCain's tormentors beat him senseless in the interrogation room. The interrogators were usually officers and the most brutal to the prisoners.

Then there were the younger turnkeys, many still in their early teens, who supervised the prisoners' daily routines. They would let the men out of their cells to eat their meals or to bathe and then lock them back in when they finished.

Last were those named "gun guards" by the prisoners, young soldiers who wandered around the camp carrying rifles on their shoulders. Many had physical handicaps or had been wounded in battle so severely that it kept them from being shipped to the front lines. It was a gun guard who was left to guard McCain's cell that night from 10 P.M. to 4 A.M., the regular shift.

After McCain awoke from his beating, he found himself still tied to his chair and in terrible pain. That's when the gun guard entered the room. The lieutenant had never talked to this man, nor even remembered making eye contact with him (something forbidden for the prisoners to do with their captors).

This young man stood inside the interrogation room for a moment, then quickly walked over to McCain. Silently, without once looking directly at or smiling at his prisoner, he loosened the ropes that bound him and left him alone in the room. Incredible relief flowed over McCain as the blood flowed back into his arms and legs. A few minutes before his shift ended, that same gun guard returned and tightened the ropes.

Without question, if that young man had been caught aiding an American prisoner, the best he could have hoped for was to be shot. In fact, the Vietnamese certainly would not have wasted a bullet; they would have made an example of him by torturing him to death for aiding the enemy. But no one knew what had happened except this nameless gun guard and Lieutenant John McCain.

Finally, the day came when McCain learned why this young man had put his life on the line to help an American prisoner of war.

It was because of Christmas Day.

On Christmas Day, the prisoners were treated to a better-than-usual dinner, including the privilege of standing outside their cells for five whole minutes to exercise or just to look at the trees and sky. When you're locked inside a small cell for days at a time, a five-minute stretch is better than opening a room chock-full of presents. That's when the same gun guard who had risked his life to loosen McCain's ropes approached the American. McCain writes,

He walked up and stood silently next to me. Again, he didn't smile or look at me. He just stared at the ground in front of us. After a few moments had passed he rather nonchalantly used his sandaled foot to draw a cross in the dirt. We both stood wordlessly looking at the cross until, after a minute or two, he rubbed it out and walked away.

Where does a person get the strength to be there for another individual made in God's image, especially for someone he may not even know? How can you be there even for an enemy?

You get such power from the cross. You find the strength to serve people with your eyes and heart—and perhaps even risk your life for another—in the shadow of the cross.

A simple cross, drawn in the dirt by a filthy sandal, might have gone unnoticed by others…but you can bet the One whose birthday was celebrated that Christmas Day saw the young man draw that cross and said, "Well done."

Wouldn't you like to hear the same words? Wouldn't you like the God of the universe to speak the thrilling phrase "Well done" into your ears after he watches your eyes and heart be there for others?

If it's possible for an anonymous Vietnamese gun guard to be there for an American prisoner of war, it's possible for you and me.

In fact, it's our great privilege.

The Clincher

There's a well-known children's book that I can't stand to read.

It's not that the book is poorly written or that its message isn't wonderfully touching. It's simply that it's so *sad*. In every attempt I've made to read it to my own daughters, I have yet to reach the last page. In fact, I barely get past the first page.

It's the story of a beloved baby boy and a mother who knew how to be there for him forever…from the first day she brought him home. She held him, slowly rocked him, and sang to him, "I'll love you forever."

The days march into years and the little boy becomes a full-grown son, full of life and with a family of his own. In time his beloved mother grows old and sick, and now is dying. Filled with love for his mother and overflowing with gratefulness for the incredible security he'd gained from her simple song, he gives her the best gift he can think to offer.

He sings back to her the words of her lullaby…only modified to include his own sense of forever. He goes to his mother, picks her up, rocks her back and forth, and sings to her, "I'll love you forever."

My own mother was too frail, too broken, in too much pain at the end of her life for me to hold her in my arms and sing to her. But I did hold her hands that night and pray for her and brush back her fine, graying hair from her soft, wet, fevered brow. Between the tears, when I could keep my voice steady enough, I'd whisper to her that on that night and for always, I'd love her. I'd love her *forever*—just as she had always loved me.

I mentioned at the beginning of this book that I first saw what it meant to be there by looking at my mother. That's absolutely true. It was in watching her that I learned how a finite person can impart a piece of *forever* to someone they truly love—a crucial mark of what it means to be there.

I tried one final time last night to struggle through the words, "I'll love you forever, I'll like you for always" with the kids…and once more I couldn't get through the book. But I think I can stop trying now. Kari, my wise, practical teenager, hugged me, shook her pretty head at her senti-mental dad, and let me off the hook *forever.*

"Daddy, don't cry," she said. "You don't have to read us that book. We know you'll love us forever. And I know Grandma loved you, too."

Can you believe me when I tell you the lump in my throat still hasn't disappeared?

Forever is the clincher when it comes to the choice to be there for others. And although "family" is the setting for this children's book (and for my release from it), the idea of *forever* that it illustrates applies equally well to our commitment to be there for the unloved and underprivileged men and women and children who live in our communities.

When Jesus told us to "work...until I come back" (Luke 19:13, NIV), who can deny that he was thinking at least in part about our work with the poor and needy? James certainly thought that was in his Lord's mind, for he wrote, "Religion that God our Father accepts as pure and faultless is this: to look after orphans and widows in their distress" (James 1:27, NIV).

And how long are we to so engage ourselves? Again, Jesus gave us a big clue when he told his disciples, "The poor you have with you *always*" (Matthew 26:11).

For those of us with eyes to see and a heart to respond, that translates to making ourselves available to be there forever.

And Jesus says, "I tell you the truth, whatever you did for one of the least of these brothers of mine, you did for me" (Matthew 25:40, NIV).

A Personal Application Project

It's time for another personal assignment. It involves answering a question:

Whose shoes need shining in your world today?

Perhaps it's some little, toddler-size 3 shoes standing impatiently in front of the rescue mission downtown. Does the young owner of those shoes need you to quit being so distracted with work or maintaining a perfectly picked up house and instead be there for her with your whole heart and mind and attention? Can you, like Albert Lexie, put your name on her?

Or perhaps it's some teenager's scruffy tennis shoes that would shine up a bit if you offered to be a mentor just for him. Or an old pair of slippers that have been longing for a home visit from *someone*.

Individuals in your community need your name to be there for them. Perhaps it's a tired widow whose shoes need buffing with your words of continued encouragement after she's spent yet another frustrating day looking for a job. Is your name on some shoes that God has placed in your neighborhood?

I think shining shoes is a wonderful metaphor for what it means to be there for someone. That's because celebrities don't get down on their knees to shine shoes, but servants do. Celebrities don't focus on making *other* people look better to the world, but servants do. Shining shoes may get your hands rough and stained, but we're called to remember the Cross and to follow those nail-pierced hands.

Albert Lexie is a hero today because he picked up his cross and followed Jesus into a hospital full of sick children. There he decided, by God's strength, to be there forever for those children and to put his name on each one by giving of his whole self...one little pair of shoes at a time.

So I ask again: Whose shoes need shining in your world today?

PART FOUR

Warning: Being There Isn't Risk-Free

On the canvas of what it means to be there, dark colors appear right alongside the bright, showy ones. These are the shadows brushed in from the side that highlight the bright sunshine—contrasting shades that give depth and movement and life…and sometimes even hide muted shapes or pictures.

I'll start wrapping up our look at what it means to be there with the following legalese warning label. It's written in my best attempt at lawyer talk, like the advisory tacked on at the end of a commercial. To get the right idea, read the warning as fast as you can without taking a breath:

> **Warning!**
> **Following God's example and choosing to have your name, eyes, and heart be there forever for others will result in dramatic changes in your life and the lives of those around you. Symptoms may include great joy, fulfillment, sacrifice, and increased sensitivity—but also a broken heart.**

I show this warning label to you only because its message is true. When you really invest yourself in helping, encouraging, fighting for, and loving someone—choosing to be there for them even against great odds—you will probably end up with a heart full of joy, but you'll also be setting yourself up for a broken heart. That's the risk of really loving someone with God's kind of love, the name-eyes-heart-forever be-there kind of love.

I've mentioned what an impact the Monet exhibit had on my family. Since then I've read a good bit about Claude Monet, and in doing so, I discovered why I think he was able to make the lilies seem to float on his pond. It has to do with the dark paint blended into what it means to be there.

It has been said by many that most great artists have found inspiration in suffering. Maybe it was the pain of losing a job, of enduring health problems, or of losing a child. Often pain helped these artists to somehow weave into their works great emotion. Paradoxically, pain and even death have added life and beauty and reality to many a painter's work.

Compared to most artists, Monet didn't know much about suffering. He was rich at a time when most impressionist artists starved. He enjoyed a devoted wife and children and a palatial home that is still open for tours. Monet had the money to create one of the grandest gardens in all of France—which really means, in all the world.

It was in his garden that Monet painted each day, letting the light and season and sound influence him. Sounds pretty low stress and low pain, doesn't it? But as I read more about him, I discovered that many of his greatest paintings were completed in that garden between 1913 and 1918.

Do those dates sound familiar?

During those awful years the birds often fell silent in Monet's garden, hushed by the gunfire of World War I just outside his garden walls. In fact, the gravelike trenches that marked the front lines and took nearly a million lives in that terrible war were at one point dug less than ten miles from Monet's front door.

It was during that time of death to nearly 1.4 million of his country-men—a catastrophe taking place just a few miles away—that Monet created pictures so full of life.

Why this art history lesson?

Because I promised that I'd show you how the Master Painter's hand has blended two distinct shades into one stunning picture of what it means to be there. Muted shades are deftly incorporated into the canvas of these two words. Yet somehow they don't muddle the image, but actually give us a brilliantly clear picture of what it looks like to really be there for others.

So take another step back from the painting and consider how the Master Artist uses even dark colors to emphasize the beauty of his sunrise.

17 | *Broken Hearts Club*

Do you remember the end of *The Wizard of Oz*? After their long, perilous journey, the Scarecrow, the Cowardly Lion, and the Tin Man were all presented their heart's desire. For the Tin Man, acquiring a heart seemed to be the end of the rainbow. Now, at long last, the Great Oz himself would present him with a watch shaped like a heart.

"It ticks!" he gasps in surprise.

Then full of joy, he places his new heart inside his formerly hollow chest of tin. In a similar atmosphere of celebration, the Scarecrow is presented with a Doctor of Thinkology degree, and the Cowardly Lion receives a shiny medal for courage.

But when it's time for Dorothy to receive her heart's desire and return to Kansas, do you remember the Tin Man's parting words? Dorothy hugs him, tells him good-bye, then sees his tears and gently scolds him, "Don't cry. You'll rust yourself."

And the Tin Man answers, "Now I know I have a heart...*because it's breaking.*"

One way to tell how much you have been there for someone is to feel your heart break when they move on or pass away. I won't kid you; if you decide to really be there for someone else, the day may well come when you look around to find your loved one is no longer "there" at all. And the deeper the connection, the greater the pain.

No matter how godly you may be.

The Bible's Broken Hearts Club

It's easy to "love" someone in the abstract, but it's quite another thing to choose to be there for another with your name, eyes, heart, and to do so forever. When you make that choice, you open yourself up to all kinds of pain that you could never even guess at otherwise.

Some of the godliest figures in the Bible made exactly that painful discovery firsthand.

Job, a man whom God himself described as "blameless and upright, a man who fears God and shuns evil," could hardly contain himself when his closest associates deserted him in his deepest hour of need. "My kinsmen have gone away," he lamented, "my friends have forgotten me. My guests and my maidservants count me a stranger; they look upon me as an alien. I summon my servant, but he does not answer, though I beg him with my own mouth. My breath is offensive to my wife; I am loathsome to my own brothers. Even the little boys scorn me; when I appear, they ridicule me. All my intimate friends detest me; those I love have turned against me" (Job 19:14-19, NIV).

David, who knew God regarded him as the apple of his eye (Psalm 17:8), also knew times of despairing solitude so fierce that he could cry out, "I am the utter contempt of my neighbors; I am a dread to my friends—those who see me on the street flee from me. I am forgotten by them as though I were dead; I have become like broken pottery" (Psalm 31:11-12, NIV).

Heman, an honored temple musician, wrote what is undoubtedly the darkest psalm in our Bibles. He ends his dirge by complaining to God,

"You have taken my companions and loved ones from me; the darkness is my closest friend" (Psalm 88:18, NIV).

Jeremiah the prophet knew all about shedding tears from relationships disturbed by sin or distance. He told the Lord, "All my friends are waiting for me to slip, saying, 'Perhaps he will be deceived; then we will prevail over him and take our revenge on him' " (Jeremiah 20:10, NIV).

The elders of the church at Ephesus suffered broken hearts when it was time for their friend and mentor to leave them. Luke says, "They all wept as they embraced him and kissed him. What grieved them most was his statement that they would never see his face again" (Acts 20:37-38, NIV).

Paul the apostle knew the sting of discouragement when, toward the end of his life, he found himself all alone. "Everyone in the province of Asia has deserted me," he told his young friend Timothy. "Demas...has deserted me and has gone to Thessalonica. Crescens has gone to Galatia, and Titus to Dalmatia. Only Luke is with me" (2 Timothy 1:15; 4:10-11, NIV).

Jesus himself wept when his dear friend, Lazarus, died (John 11:35). And his heart broke yet again when, at his arrest, his disciples "deserted him and fled," just like sheep scattering before a wolf (Matthew 26:31,56, NIV).

Godliness is no vaccine against a heart broken over the loss of a departing loved one. In fact, the more godly you are and the more deeply you love, the greater may be your sense of loss when the one for whom you chose to be there is no longer "there."

For me, I remember two broken hearts sitting around the same old kitchen table...

One Last Time

The year was 1972. I'd been up almost all night, first saying good-bye to my few remaining high-school friends, and then packing for college myself. Finally, I sat at our old kitchen table with my mother, enjoying her famous pancakes one last time before climbing into my jam-packed car.

As I sat there, a flood of emotions hit me. My mother had purchased that table at an auction when we first moved into our house. That was back in 1957 when I was five years old. She bought the table because it fit perfectly in our small dining area next to a large kitchen window. From anywhere at the table, you enjoyed a commanding view of the front yard. And for almost two decades, it served as the unofficial meeting place of the Trent family.

In grade school I sat there at countless dinners. We three boys would be laughing and chattering about our day while my mother and grand-mother scurried back and forth to keep bottomless plates filled. For a year before his death, my grandfather quietly presided over the chaos engulf-ing that table. I can still remember playing in the front yard and looking up to see Grandfather sitting at the table, sipping his coffee, smoking his pipe, doing his crossword puzzle, and giving us a smile and a wave of his hand.

In high school that table became the place where I could sit with my mother anytime, day or night. There she would patiently listen to what-ever crisis or problem I was having in school or with the girls I wanted to date. Always she would be there for us in every sense of those words.

That old table proudly displayed birthday cards as we grew older, and it solemnly bore the flowers we brought home from the funeral home when my grandfather and then my aunt were laid to rest.

Over the years, more chairs began to empty. My older brother, Joe, married and began a home of his own. My grandmother went to live with my aunt, and my twin brother, Jeff, left for a different college. Now it was down to just Mom and me, sitting at that table one last time.

I remember how well I thought she was handling that particular morning, even to the very instant I was all packed up and ready to drive away to college. I'd be the last one to leave, leaving Mom to sit at that table all alone. Yet there were no tears that morning. No dimming of her always-present smile. Just that nonstop encouragement that had calmed my fears since I was a child and always made me feel as though I could accomplish anything I set my mind to. Things like driving a thousand miles alone over the next two days to attend a new college, a foreign place where I didn't know a single soul.

I finished breakfast, hugged the best mom in the world, and confidently strode to my '64 forest green Volkswagen. Every square inch was crammed with "important stuff" for college—which meant everything from my legendary record collection to my seldom-used razor. I jumped inside, fired up the engine, and drove off with a wave and a smile.

I was on my way. Nothing would stop me now. Nothing, that is, except driving into the rising sun for a few minutes. *Wait a minute,* I thought, *I've forgotten my sunglasses on the nightstand!*

In Arizona, if you start off on a trip to the store, much less across the country, the sun won't let you forget something as important as shades. So blinking my eyes, I turned the car around, drove back into the driveway, and walked in to find my mother still sitting at the kitchen table...*crying*.

All morning she had managed to keep a stiff upper lip, holding her emotions in check at seeing her last son leave home. But when I walked back in the door unexpectedly, all that changed. For a moment an awkward silence reigned as I stood there and saw her tears—and then we both lost it. We each sat at that table, so crowded with memories, and hugged each other, hearts full of love and broken at the same time...just like the Tin Man's.

And just like yours, too, if you choose to be there for someone else, forever, with all your heart and your eyes and all that your name represents.

One Promise

I can't promise you that your heart won't be broken if you decide to really, truly, be there for others. In fact, I think at some point, it will be. But I can promise you that it will be worth every tear, even if the time comes when you lose that person, whether to distance or disease or desertion.

Because Jesus has irrevocably chosen to be there for us, we'll meet our loved ones again in a new land where there will be no more tears, no more sorrow, and no more sickness. And when you see Jesus face to face and everything else that seemed so important fades away, you'll be so glad you spent your time on earth to be there for others…just as he did.

18 | *The Worst Pain in the World*

Do you know what it's like to really need someone to be there for you at a dark, pain-wrapped moment in your life? Perhaps there's a person you worked with, stayed up late helping time after time, prayed for, and believed was in your inner circle of closest friends.

But then the time came when you needed him or her...really needed that friend...and he or she seemed as responsive to your need as someone fast asleep.

Jesus can relate.

Tears in a Garden

In a word-association test, the word *garden* normally brings up thoughts of flowers, rich, moist earth, and warm summer days. The word *garden* usually doesn't elicit thoughts of betrayal, fear, abandonment, and death.

That is, until you link the word *Gethsemane* with *garden*.

Across a ravine, within easy walking distance of the temple, lay the Garden of Gethsemane. There a series of events would take place that would culminate in Jesus' death. And there he would suffer the single worst night of his life.

Just hours before Jesus was betrayed, the first dark brush strokes were added to the canvas known as Calvary.

> Then Jesus came with them to a place called Gethsemane,
> and said to His disciples, "Sit here while I go over there
> and pray." And He took with Him Peter and the two sons
> of Zebedee, and began to be grieved and distressed. Then
> He said to them, "My soul is deeply grieved, to the point
> of death; remain here and keep watch with Me."
> (Matthew 26:36-38)

The word *grieved* literally means to be "wrapped in pain," while the word *distressed* means "to be anxious." Jesus didn't leave his friends guessing about the depth of the struggle he faced. He told Peter and the others that he was not only "grieved," but he was "*deeply* grieved," even wrapped in pain. Would they please be there for him that night?

> And He went a little beyond them, and fell on His face
> and prayed, saying, "My Father, if it is possible, let this cup
> pass from Me; yet not as I will, but as Thou wilt." And He
> came to the disciples and found them sleeping, and said to
> Peter, "So, you men could not keep watch with Me for one
> hour?" (26:39-40)

Asking again for their support, Jesus goes away a second time…and then a third. But it's the same sad story each go-round. Those he was closest to, those who had received the most from him, those he had put his name and eyes and heart on forever—they should have been there when he really needed them, if only for an hour.

But they weren't. They repaid our Lord's love and commitment with snores and silence.

Nevertheless, Jesus was hardly surprised by their actions. Earlier that night he had predicted as much. Just before he and his disciples had left the Upper Room and walked to Gethsemane, Peter loudly proclaimed that even if everyone else proved false as a friend, he'd be there for Jesus forever, through thick or thin. "Even if I have to die with You, I will not deny You," Peter boasted.

Jesus listened to his bravado and calmly replied, "Truly I say to you that this very night, before a cock crows, you shall deny Me three times" (26:34).

Betrayal, the Darkest of Colors

That terrible night Peter did indeed run away with the rest of the disciples after putting up a halfhearted defense of his Master. But to his credit, a little later he mustered up his courage and followed his friend (at a distance) into the courtyard of the high priest. It was there, in the cold hours of the night, that Peter stood and warmed himself over a charcoal fire.

> Now the slaves and the officers were standing there, having made a charcoal fire, for it was cold and they were warming themselves; and Peter also was with them, standing and warming himself. (John 18:18)

Peter found warmth in the enemy camp that night—but there would be no warmth for Jesus. Already his friends had failed to console Jesus, and false witnesses had accused him. Now one of his very best friends would deny him right to his face. And not once, but three times, just as Jesus had said he would.

> The slave-girl therefore who kept the door said to Peter, "You are not also one of this man's disciples, are you?" He said, "I am not." (18:17)

But Peter aroused the suspicions of the officers around the fire.

> Now Simon Peter was standing and warming himself. They said therefore to him, "You are not also one of His disciples, are you?" He denied it, and said, "I am not." (18:25)

And then comes the third time.

> One of the slaves of the high priest…said, "Did I not see you in the garden with Him?" Peter therefore denied it again; and immediately a cock crowed. (18:26-27)

As if the crowing of the rooster weren't enough to announce Peter's denial, the Gospel of Luke tells us the rest of the story: "And the Lord turned and looked at Peter" (Luke 22:61).

Now, if you were Peter, how would you have felt at that awful moment? Not only did the rooster give you a screaming reminder of Christ's prophecy, but immediately after your lying lips betrayed your friend, you turned around to see his eyes gazing into your own. You know he overheard you swearing and cursing that you didn't even *know* him and that he meant nothing to you.

Do you think Peter ever forgot the hurt and sorrow he put in Jesus' eyes? It was then, as he was flooded by the pain he'd caused, that he went out and wept bitterly.

Yes, our Lord knew all about betrayal. Not just from Judas, who for thirty pieces of silver turned on his friend, wickedly emphasizing his treachery with a kiss. But now from one of his very best friends, Peter, one of the inner circle, the acknowledged leader of them all.

Cut to the Quick

Betrayal is one of the risks you take when you decide to be there for others.

Just ask Jim about that.

Jim was asked to join a small start-up company that needed a number-two man. He jumped at the chance, not only because it gave him the freedom to use his gifts, but also because one of his very best friends was the number-one man—in fact, the guy who hired him. It was like going to work for your brother, Jim told everyone, and he threw his whole heart into building "their" company.

Jim's first week on the job, he set up a meeting that landed the company a contract that paid his entire salary for the next two years. During the whole time Jim worked with his friend, he never cost the company a dime, generated more than a dozen new profitable products and contracts, and plowed all the revenues back into growing the company.

And it wasn't only at work that Jim was there for his friend.

When his partner's son was involved in a car wreck, Jim made it to the hospital before any of the boy's family members and stayed with him until after midnight. He went out of his way to help his friend's other children and treated the man's wife with respect and high regard as well.

Then came the day *Jim* needed help...

During a two-week period just before Christmas, Jim's father and mother were both admitted to the hospital. His mother would recover, but his father wouldn't. During the three weeks his father clung to life and the three months his mother convalesced, Jim's parents received not a single card, visit, or call from his "best friend." At his father's funeral, only one person from the office showed up, and it wasn't Jim's friend. In fact, the only call Jim received from his partner on the day of the funeral was to check on the status of a project, not on the state of Jim's wounded heart.

Jim had poured himself into serving and helping and supporting his friend's family and trying to be there for him. But when the time came that Jim needed comfort and support, it was as if his friend deliberately rolled over and went to sleep. (And no, the man's name wasn't Peter.)

Not long after Jim's father died, his partner received an "offer he couldn't refuse" to sell the company to a group of out-of-town investors. The man never discussed his plans with Jim after the initial meetings, because the "money people" had made it clear there would be no place in the new digs for his old partner. And after all, Jim's boss reasoned, the two of them had never actually signed any papers between them. Technically, it wasn't a partnership like Jim had been told a hundred times. Legally, his boss could pack up and sell out.

Which is exactly what he did.

So after nearly a decade of working to create what he thought was job security, Jim found himself unemployed. His "friend" sold out and moved away in less than three months. Oh, Jim got a severance package. He received a paycheck those last three months for fulfilling his full-time job responsibilities, even while scrambling to find another job. And he got to listen to his best friend and boss cut him to the quick with a purposeful, parting shot, spoken right to his face: "This company grew because of *me*. You never were a good salesman."

Ten years of tangible, traceable, bottom-line building efforts were erased by his boss's words—as if Jim had never been there at all. Those words cut more deeply than being cut out of a future with the company or being cut loose…because they came from a friend.

No Wound So Painful and Yet…

When you decide to be there for someone forever, with all your heart and your eyes and your name, there's no guarantee that one day you won't find yourself abandoned and betrayed.

Is there any wound so painful as a betrayal? Is there an injury so excruciating as a friend who turns on you? No one gets so close to the center of your heart as a trusted friend, and therefore no hurt can compare to the spear thrust of treachery at the hands of a friend.

When as an old man the apostle Paul was betrayed by those he thought were his friends, his broken heart grieved. "At my first defense," he wrote, "no one came to my support, but everyone deserted me." That's not an easy blow to take—but a man or woman determined to follow the example set by God finds a way to take it. Paul took it like this, saying of his deserters, "May it not be counted against them" (2 Timothy 4:16).

Amazing, isn't it? But not so amazing that it's a one-of-a-kind occurrence. Stephen, the first martyr of the church, with his last breath cried out to God on behalf of those who were stoning him, "Lord, do not hold this sin against them" (Acts 7:60).

Both Paul and Stephen had learned well from their Lord and Savior, Jesus Christ, who set the standard for astonishing responses to betrayal. On the cross our Master prayed for those who crucified him, "Father, forgive them; for they do not know what they are doing" (Luke 23:34).

Does betrayal hurt? More than anything.

And yet, when God is involved, not even betrayal has the last word.

Peter, remember, was restored to fellowship with Christ and became a courageous leader of the early church.

And sitting there guarding the coats of the men who stoned Stephen was a man named Saul, soon to be known as Paul the apostle. The Lord heard Stephen's dying prayer, and Paul was part of his answer.

The possibility of betrayal is no reason to withhold our love, to refuse to be there for others. Betrayal hurts, surely. And it leaves deep scars (consider Stephen's broken body, Paul's whiplashed back, and Jesus' pierced hands, feet, and side).

But somehow, in the amazing plan of God, even the dark colors of betrayal can be skillfully worked into a painting bursting with life and light and redemption.

My friend, it's worth it to be there for others, even at the risk of betrayal. Because you just never know when that very betrayal will uncover another Peter or another Paul. Only God knows that ahead of time—and he wants us to make the discovery on our own.

Are you willing?

PART FIVE

Barriers to Being There

You've read page after page of encouragement to be there, despite the possible heartache that can come with truly loving and connecting with others. But a broken heart isn't the only thing that can stop someone from being there. There are actually a number of barriers that can keep even the most enthusiastic "climber" from reaching new heights.

Several years ago, on a rainy August day, two young adventurers decided to scale the 14,942-foot Mount Dom, near Zermatt, Switzerland. Young and relatively inexperienced, they felt confident in their mountain-climbing abilities. Too confident, it turned out.

At noon they boldly strode forth. Their goal was a halfway house called the "high hut," which was staffed by the Swiss Alpine Club. There they could safely spend the night before tackling the icy summit the next morning. But soon after they left, rain began falling, and the temperature began to drop significantly as well. In a short time, their inadequate clothing was soaked through.

At 6:00 P.M. the rain suddenly turned to snow. By 7:00 P.M. the trail was nearly impossible to see. By 8:00 P.M. they were lost...and in life-threatening trouble. Darkness was falling; they were soaked, shivering, and heading toward hypothermia. They had no way of knowing if they were still headed toward the high hut, and they had no tent or sleeping bags in which to escape the cold.

And then something miraculous happened. From a great distance away, a tiny light began to flicker. The faint light looked as bright as a lighthouse beacon to those two shivering, frightened young men. Where did it come from? Before retiring for the night, the keeper of Mount Dom's high hut had decided to place a kerosene lamp next to the door— just in case a beacon might be needed by anyone caught in the worsening storm.

In many ways, that story captures the essence of this section, "Barriers to Being There." Learning about the life-changing effects of putting our name, eyes, and heart on our loved ones can cause us to head up the mountain with great excitement and confidence. But along the way there will be trials and stumbles. Just one look at the morning paper tells us that we're walking into a fallen world full of gathering darkness.

In this next section, you'll discover there is a way around and through those common barriers to being there. That way of escape is none other than the Light of the World—Jesus—the One who alone can save, guide, and keep us safe and warm, both now and forever. The apostle Matthew tells us, "The people who were sitting in darkness saw a great light" (Matthew 4:16). The apostle Peter tells us, "You do well to pay attention as to a lamp shining in a dark place" (2 Peter 1:19). And the psalmist tells us God's Word is "a lamp to my feet, and a light to my path" (Psalm 119:105).

As you read about the barriers that can make the going tough, realize that Jesus has already been there, done that, faced that trial or temptation—and has come out on top. Which is just where he's calling us to go.

19 | *The Flight of the Hooded Falcon*
(and other counterfeits that keep us from being there)

I nestled into the cockpit of the F-16 like I was trying to squeeze into a tight-fitting pair of shoes. The senior flight officer instructing me, in this case my good friend Major Bo McGowan of the 56th Fighter Wing, had warned me of the tight fit. He'd already spent nearly an hour with us in the ready room where we went over basic flight procedures, safety issues, the key instruments of the space-age heads-up display on the windshield screen, and our mission plan.

Our preflight training over, we walked to our plane—beautiful, sleek, deadly. Like a long silver Corvette, it looked as if it were speeding even as it sat on the ground. It was a perfect day as I climbed up the ladder, eased into the cockpit, and adjusted my helmet. Major Bo gave last-minute instructions, but nerves kept me from concentrating on what he said.

After I was buttoned up inside the cockpit, Major Bo's voice boomed clear and strong from the tiny speaker in my helmet. Following his instructions, I powered up the warship…taxied to the runway…and then was cleared to head out on my first solo flight in the most sophisticated and deadly combat aircraft in the world: the F-16 Flying Falcon. With the engine screaming, I eased off the air brakes and was slammed back in my seat at the same time I shot forward. With just the hint of movement, I pulled back on the short toggle stick and was airborne.

I was flying!

The desert over Luke Air Force Base dropped beneath me as I shot up into the clouds. With the heads-up display in front of me, all my vital instruments, navigation, radar, and weapons data appear right there at eye-level. In a heartbeat I was over Casa Grande, Arizona—a trip that would have taken over an hour in my truck. Then I turned back toward Luke Airfield, landed, took off again, flew actual combat scenarios, and finally heard Major Bo's voice say...

"Okay, Ace. Mission accomplished. *It's Laura's turn now.*"

I did as ordered, landed the plane, and let my daughter (who was seven at the time) climb into the cockpit and take her turn at protecting the Free World.

Did I forget to mention that the F-16 I flew was the famous Hooded Falcon? The most advanced, full-motion, full-display, combat flight *simulator* in the world?

But I swear, it *wasn't* a simulator when I was inside. It was real!

The hydraulics that moved the seat, as well as the actual (albeit partial) fuselage of the plane a pilot sits in, gives the sensation of speed and of pitching in the air. I bumped through turbulence streaking through clouds and felt the wheels thump when I touched down. (Although "bumped down" would be more accurate.) Controllers made the weather beautiful or stormy for me, and the camera image that literally surrounded me as I took off over the desert is real.

Believe me, I grew up in Arizona and I know desert. This was *real.* So was the tension inside the cockpit when we did air combat and those enemy fighters shot by like a blur.

It was *real,* I tell you. *I really did fly the F-16!*

(Sorry, taxpayers, but I cratered twice, racking up a measly $40 million in lost aircraft.)

At least my experience was "real" if you consider reality to be tricking your senses into thinking you've really been there in combat or at takeoff or in a crash landing. My time in the cockpit was real in the same sense that too many people think they're really being there for the Lord and for their loved ones.

Reality Check

Image and trickery isn't the same as substance and truth—no matter what your feelings or senses or friends may say.

That's the problem with our virtual-reality world, where Nintendo scenes have become almost as real as real life. We get tricked into thinking that we're actually doing something that we're not. In our mind we can see it, but in the actual, tangible, old-fashioned kind of reality that requires both truth and substance (instead of a mere image), we're only kidding ourselves.

Which is why we need a reality check before we call ourselves an F-16 pilot...or before we assume we're already being there for others.

How real is your commitment to others?

Are your name, eyes, and heart really on the Lord and your loved ones? When I was flying that day, it seemed so real inside my little cocoon. But my whole family was standing outside the simulator, watching reality. As long as I stayed in my little, artificial world—relying on Major Bo and two computer experts working constantly to make that artificial reality seem real—I could fly! But Cindy, Kari, Laura, and especially Major Bo (who has flown F-16s in harm's way in actual combat) knew it was little more than a game. I could think what I wanted, but my wings weren't real.

That's what this chapter is about. It's about taking an honest look at four virtual reality hangouts that can convince people they're really soaring—when in fact they're stuck in a simulator that will never get off the ground.

What follows are four reality checks. Call them "safety checks" if you'd like. After all, it never hurts to do safety checks before you take off and fly.

The Safety Check of Greatness

While you're waiting in line at Starbucks for your next mocha, just listen to the conversations taking place around you. Chances are they're all about 401(k)s, hot stock tips, great sales, and low mortgage rates. It's all about the things that mark someone today as "great."

While the topic of 401(k)s wouldn't come up among the disciples, their own definition of greatness was all they could talk about one day. Jesus warned them away from the impostor that enchanted them and toward the greatness that comes only from "being there."

> And they came to Capernaum; and when He was in the
> house, He began to question them, "What were you dis-
> cussing on the way?" But they kept silent, for on the way
> they had discussed with one another which of them was
> the greatest. (Mark 9:33-34)

At this time in Christ's ministry the popularity gauge had reached its high point. Jesus' disciples knew they were "somebodies" because they were the disciples of Someone with so much potential and popular appeal.

With his ratings sky-high, Jesus had a rich future before him. The disciples were already talking about their slice of the pie.

Jesus could be king of Israel—others had said as much. He could call down legions of angels to fight for him and become the greatest general of all time. He could heal the sick and raise the dead and take over the top medical spots in the land. And *they* were his close companions. If anyone stood to profit from proximity to so much greatness, it was them. And that's just what they were talking about.

Who would be the greatest? Who among them would end up with the most boats or houses or land? Who would achieve the most? Be worth the most? Be able to brag the longest at their twenty-year synagogue school reunion? Those are the kind of conversations that go on at Starbucks today, and they apparently had been going on between the disciples. It was all about wanting more—more fame, more power, more money, more land, more clothing, more something.

But having more fails the safety check.

Jesus set them straight on that point when he did something all teachers did back then when they wanted their words to be "official." He sat down. It was like saying, "Listen, class, this will be on an upcoming test!"

> And sitting down, He called the twelve and said to them, "If any one wants to be first, he shall be last of all, and servant of all." And taking a child, He stood him in the midst of them; and taking him in His arms, He said to them, "Whoever receives one child like this in My name is receiving Me; and whoever receives Me is not receiving Me, but Him who sent Me." (9:35-37)

Jesus grounds their flights of fancy by rejecting the idea that greatness is all about power or prestige or things. He tells them that greatness comes from being a servant. Even a person with no power, little prestige, and few things can be great if he puts love into shoe leather, like an Albert Lexie. True greatness comes in helping, in anticipating needs, in being on call, and in lending a hand. Those are the sorts of things servants do.

To make sure his disciples got the point, Jesus set a solitary child in their midst—not lots of children, like the time the Savior beckoned many to come to him for hugs and blessings, but a single child. Jesus wanted to make a clear point, underscored by his words.

To quote the Trent Amplified Bible Commentary on what Jesus said and did here, it was as if Jesus told them, "This is it. This is the path to real greatness. Do you really want to be in first place? Have the most? Get the most honor when it's all said and done? Then become the absolute best servant you can be. Seek to meet people's needs in the present—that's the place to start. Begin by choosing to 'be there' for someone who needs you—like this one precious child I'm holding in my arms and blessing.

"Do you really want to be great? Then start by blessing one child."

Our world fails this safety check because it believes greatness is all about hoarding more money, earning higher degrees, building bigger houses, buying faster roadsters, finding better lovers, and taking longer cruises to Cabo.

But none of those things ever get off the ground.

I recently spoke with a wife whose husband takes her all over the world, yet who is never really there with her. Even when they're sitting down to dinner at a fancy restaurant in some exotic locale, he never looks her in the eyes but continuously scans the room to see what "players" might be walking in the door. She's dying inside because even though he's there physically, he's light-years away emotionally, mentally, and spiritually. He's so disconnected from his family's daily life that he doesn't even know what day the trashmen come. He's always smiling, but never connecting. He doesn't seem to understand that being there for his family does not mean taking them places. He's been seduced by this world's idea of greatness.

True greatness comes by being there for our loved ones. It comes by helping even one little one who needs you. Jesus didn't tell his disciples to be there for a village; he called them to use their name and eyes and heart to bless one child.

Where is that "one child" in your own home, school, church, or neighborhood? Who is that "one child" who needs you?

Answer: The one whom God puts in front of you.

The Safety Check of Virtual Religion

Let's return to the temple for yet another lesson in what it means to be there. This time, Jesus asks for another safety check that, if disregarded, can keep us from real faith, real love, and really being there for others.

> And as He [Jesus] passed by, He saw a man blind from birth. And His disciples asked Him, saying, "Rabbi, who sinned, this man or his parents, that he should be born blind?" (John 9:1-2)

Homeless, hopeless people in Jesus' day knew just what corner to stand on to receive the most donations and handouts. They lined up next to the archway leading into Solomon's temple, looking for compassion from those on their way to church. Like bell-ringers with their buckets at Christmastime, these people knew when human hearts were most open to giving.

Right there a blind man sat, looking for no one and nothing more than a few coins. He's the lowest of the low, a man with no future and no hope. No wonder Jesus' disciples looked on his pitiful appearance and thought, *This guy is being judged for something.* So they asked the One who knows all things, "Who sinned, this man or his parents?"

That's the second safety check we must pass if we're to really, truly be there for the people in our world. Just as he shattered their counterfeit view of greatness, Jesus is about to erase his disciples' excuse for not loving and serving someone—even those with great needs and greater hurts.

"It was neither that this man sinned, nor his parents," Jesus declared, "but it was in order that the works of God might be displayed in him." And then the Master went on to refocus his disciples' mental framework so that they might be there for the people who crossed their paths.

> We must work the works of Him who sent Me, as long as
> it is day; night is coming, when no man can work. While I
> am in the world, I am the light of the world. (John 9:4-5)

It is so easy to look at those with "issues" or "deep needs" and think, *They brought it on themselves.* Or, *They're in prison for a reason.* Or, *If she hadn't had that affair, she wouldn't have lost her marriage. She's just suffering the effects of her sin.*

It's absolutely true that sin has consequences—sometimes brutal, harsh consequences. But Jesus wants his disciples to understand that many people in the world get cancer at age ten through no fault of their own; some lose their jobs unfairly when they're fifty-five; another is still falling apart two years after his spouse died, and it's not "sin," but "suffering."

If anyone should be working today to alleviate pain and bring light to dark places, it's those of us who claim to follow Jesus.

When Jesus' disciples saw the blind man, they immediately turned his plight into a theological issue. That's a pretty good strategy if you want to keep human suffering at arm's length. If you can turn a real person into an issue, then you've created an intellectual debate, nothing more. "Who sinned? The man or his parents?"

We do the same thing today when we see the homeless or hurting and immediately blame society or the lack of social programs or anything else that might keep *us* from doing something.

That kind of faith fails the second safety check.

It's the kind of faith demonstrated by the three religious leaders who showed up prior to the Good Samaritan. Their kind of faith walks right past genuine needs, even while sounding utterly pious.

Just like Mr. Dixon.

You didn't call Mr. Dixon by his first name. Not that anyone actually knew it or had ever used it as far as I could tell; his mother, perhaps. But no one at the church we attended several years ago.

Mr. Dixon was an elder at the church and served on the local board of a national ministry that takes Bibles across the country and the world. But while he would fly to Russia to pass out Bibles, he wouldn't walk across the kitchen floor to wash the dishes for his wife. While he never missed an elders' meeting, he never made it to his oldest daughter's basketball games—not a single one.

Over the years, his wife turned bitter and finally divorced him. Yet Mr. Dixon never missed a Sunday. He came with his head held high, always remembering to ask for prayers for his "straying" wife. After all, biblically he hadn't done anything wrong. His wife was the one who sinned when she moved out and filed for divorce. *He* didn't need to go into counseling; *she* did. It was *her* sin that was the problem. (Or…maybe her parents' sin?)

People like Mr. Dixon step right over the needs of others, even over their own spouse's. Why? Because they're so much like us. They want to believe that being "spiritually minded" is the same as actually meeting needs. They want to think that they can be "righteous" by blaming the collapse of a marriage on a spouse's sin, or on the blind man's parents, and never see their own problems or unwillingness to get their hands dirty.

None of us will ever truly be there for someone if we insist on shifting to the side the need to serve and help and love hurting people, while we keep up our perfect-attendance pin at our ministry board meeting.

That's simulator faith, not the real thing.

Just ask your spouse or children or people at work if you're being there for them. Like the response Jesus gave to his disciples, the answer may surprise you.

The Safety Check of Perpetual Youth

The other day I found the perfect headline to illustrate this next safety check. It's an illusion that holds so many of us back from being there for others. The headline read: "Web site trying to auction model eggs."

The accompanying article described a group of supermodels who have turned their human embryos into a high-priced commodity. For a mere $150,000, you, too, can implant one of these famous eggs in the womb of your choice. Why wait to pay a plastic surgeon when you can have perfection right out of the womb?

As silly as this sounds, the site's Web server took thousands of hits each day. We're a society that can't stand imperfection. Technology has squeezed out errors in manufacturing until "zero defects" isn't a goal; rather, it is the standard. The desire to be beautiful or thin or buff—and most of all, to look young—has become a god swallowing up the energy meant to be channeled into being there for others.

Many people are not living at the health club or jogging on the streets to keep their heart in shape so they can live longer to serve and love and be there for others. No way! Instead, it's primp time for prime time. People want to look like supermodels, and they'll sacrifice whatever it takes—time away from anyone—to get that look. And if they're not into exercise to gain beauty, they can simply join the well over two million men and women who opted for elective plastic surgery in 1999.

Look, I'm all for exercise and for looking your best (no matter what my daughters say about my outdated wardrobe). But if you think that looking better is the key to better relationships and to deeper personal connections and to being there for others, you've just failed the third safety check. And you're stuck on the ground.

Jesus put it like this:

> For this reason I say to you, do not be anxious for your life,
> as to what you shall eat, or what you shall drink; nor for
> your body, as to what you shall put on. Is not life more
> than food, and the body than clothing?... But seek first
> His kingdom and His righteousness; and all these things
> shall be added to you. (Matthew 6:25,33)

To truly be there means playing on the rug with your three-year-old. If you rush to the gym right after work because "that's when my buddies can spot me" instead of going directly home to be there for your kids while they're still awake, then you need to get new buddies. The buddies at home need you more than you need to pump iron. Find an all-night gym if you have to, get up at 5:30 A.M., buy a home gym, or wait until they're in college to exercise and then shock them by winning Mr. America after you hit fifty. But don't think that looking good at the expense of being there for your loved ones will make you look any better.

The same thing goes for the woman who spends more hours cleaning her house than caring for her family, or who runs up credit-card bills buying more makeup or new clothes to keep herself "looking great." One woman I know refuses to let her five grandchildren call her *Grandmother* because she refuses to admit she's that old. Listen, that kind of commitment to self is sin, plain and simple.

I guarantee that you won't look any worse to God if you skip a workout or wear a dress twice in order to be there for a loved one. And if you do spend time to be there for your spouse and children and grandchildren… every year you'll look better to the ones who really count.

The Safety Check of Foundation Cracks

My good friend and former seminary classmate Dr. Tony Evans recently told a wonderful story that illustrates one final safety check. It seems that the Evans family moved into a new house, and in no time cracks appeared in the ceiling. When Tony called a dry-wall repairman to fix the cracks, the man took one look at the problem and told my friend he couldn't do the job.

"Why not?" Tony asked in surprise.

"Because you don't have a crack-in-the-ceiling problem, Pastor," he replied. "You have a foundation problem."

Before any of us start slapping dry-wall mud on the ceiling of our relationships and texturing the cracks, we need to discover whether we really have a foundation problem. And if we find cracks in the foundation of our marriage or with our children, we need to start with those first. Otherwise, all our efforts to be there will come apart at the seams and be resented rather than welcomed.

If you need to, ask forgiveness of your spouse or children.

If you've hurt him, listen to the complaint of your friend.

If you've wounded her, take your rightful blame from your associate.

Remember Mr. Dixon? As long as he refused to see any needs or problems or cracks in the foundation of his life, he found no basis for reconciliation with his wife.

Being there for others can't coexist with pride. One breaks down while the other builds up. "Pride goes before destruction," we're in told in Proverbs, and "A man's pride will bring him low, but a humble spirit will obtain honor" (16:18; 29:23).

If you've hurt your spouse or children by your pride or insensitivity, then before you do anything else, stop and ask his or her forgiveness. Mend the fence before you move on.

Otherwise, you fail the fourth safety check. And you'll remain firmly chained to the ground.

The Object Is to Win

Shortly before the 1928 Olympic games, Johnny Weismuller pulled a tendon in his right leg. He feared that if he showed any pain or limped at all, his coach might put in a replacement. So for two days, Weismuller walked around in agony, trying to ignore the pain, and his leg grew worse each day.

Finally he faced up to the real problem. In his words, "My object shouldn't be to cover up my injury so I could compete, but to get healed so I could win!"

It wasn't until Weismuller admitted he wasn't perfect and took his hurts to the trainer that the heat lamps and cold rubs healed his problem. Two days later, instead of focusing on the pain in this leg or on trying to convince himself that it wasn't really there, he focused on winning an Olympic gold medal.

Which is exactly what he did.

My friend, if you have cracks in your foundation or past hurts that are still a problem, don't ignore them. That's simulator thinking, and it'll keep you on the ground instead of getting you up in the air where you really want to be.

Remember, it's always better to take our hurts to the Great Architect and ask him to help us patch up our foundation than to allow the plaster to keep falling on our head.

20 | *The Four Horsemen Go a-Haunting*

We just looked at four safety checks we need to make before trying to take to the air and soar through the friendly skies of rich relationships and deep connections.

Now I'd like to spend just a little time scanning the horizon for a quartet of hoof-pounding baddies that love to target us for haunt-and-destroy missions. And I want to say, as clearly as I can, that none of us will be there for those we love if our relationships are characterized by the four horsemen we're about to meet. Make no mistake, this fearsome foursome looks nothing like the image Solomon borrowed to praise his wife.

In fact, the very presence of these four horsemen in your life can signal that you won't be there for your loved ones in the days to come.

Four Relationship Killers

Do you want to read something scary?

Not Stephen-King-novel scary.

Really scary.

It's found in a book called *Why Marriages Succeed or Fail* by Dr. John Gottman, a professor at the University of Washington in Seattle.[1] Gottman is a Research Science Award winner from the National Institute of Mental Health who delivers this frightening declaration:

"I can predict whether a couple will divorce after watching and listening to them for just five minutes."

"What a braggart!" you might say. "What arrogance! No one knows the future except God."

Go ahead and get indignant about his statement, but understand that Gottman (a frequent guest on Focus on the Family) would agree with you that God *can* change people and he *alone* knows the future.

But that doesn't mean that in a scant five minutes of watching couples discuss an issue in his office, he can't predict with 87 percent accuracy those who are headed toward a marital cliff and near-certain destruction if certain patterns don't change.

What patterns?

Gottman breaks them down into four horsemen, drawing on the potent imagery from the book of Revelation in which the arrival of four horsemen signals the end of the world. It is Gottman's belief that if all four of these relational horsemen visit a marriage and stay—*with nothing intervening to chase them away*—then the likelihood of divorce is a statistical certainty.

While Gottman focuses solely on marriages, it's easy to see how his insights apply to all human relationships. Marriage may be the most intimate relationship possible between two people, but it's a relationship all the same. And if these four horsemen can trample a marriage into the dust, what do you think they're capable of doing to any other personal connection between two or more individuals?

Let's look briefly at these four roughriders and determine to chase them away from all of our relationships, including marriage.

The First Horseman: Criticism

Gottman isn't talking about mere complaining or correcting. When this horseman gallops into your relationships, it means a full-scale attack has been launched on a person's personality or character, achieved through flaming arrows of angry words of blame. In particular, the "shoulds" come out.

"You should have known I don't like that kind of coffee."

"Everyone but you knows that you shouldn't park so close to another car."

This horseman never gives out constructive comments, nor does he point out issues or problems in a constructive way. We're talking hot, scalding criticism.

"You oaf, you never do anything right."

"I can't stand to look at your sorry excuse for a face."

"You should have left hours ago. Can't you ever get anything straight?"

Spend too much time in the company of this horseman, and all hope for deep connections and satisfying relationships will go riding pell-mell into the wilderness.

The Second Horseman: Contempt

In Gottman's words, "What separates contempt from criticism is the intention to insult and psychologically abuse your partner." This horseman leaves whatever issue is being discussed to start attacking the other person.

"You arrogant fool, what do you know?"

"How stupid can you be?"

"I never knew incompetence until I met you."

"There you go again, you dummy."

This horseman is all about hurting with words, not using words to picture a needed change or a positive future. His sword is razor sharp, his arrows carry poisoned tips, and the relationship that doesn't quickly chase him away has little chance of survival.

The Third Horseman: Defensiveness

This evil rider is an expert at subjecting his victims to what I like to call emotional sunburn.

Have you ever gone water skiing on a Saturday and then attended your Sunday-school class on Sunday? Guaranteed, at least a hundred people (even if the class seats only fifteen), will come up and slap you on the back with an enthusiastic, "Hello! How are you doing this fine morning?"

If you have a serious sunburn, just the thought of someone lifting his hand to slap you on the back can make you flinch. This third horseman leaves its prey so defensive that nearly every word or action brings a hypersensitive response. Ask a simple question, and you'll likely get,

"What do you want *now?*"

"Why can't you just leave me alone?"

"What—do you think *you're* perfect?"

"Get off my case!"

This horseman represents the emotional walls we put up in order to keep from being hurt. But in the process, we block our ability to deal with issues in a positive way.

The Fourth Horseman: Stonewalling

You recognize this rider at work when you notice that someone who should be listening instead becomes a stone wall.

Whenever some sensitive issue arises, instantly the barriers go up. All willingness to engage, interact, pray about something, talk it through, or call for help turns into a cold, hard stone wall that says,

"I'm not changing."

"I'm not talking about it."

"I refuse to discuss that."

"I'm not doing anything about it—and that's final!"

This horseman might be the most silent of the lot, but don't imagine that makes him any less dangerous. He's the stealth fighter of the four, the ninja assassin who kills without a sound. Often he needs no words at all to accomplish his deadly work. And before anyone knows he has cantered into town, the corpse is rotting under a noontime sun.

Finding Hope While There's Still Time

If these four horsemen are allowed to remain in a relationship over time, death is the almost certain result.

Death of a friendship.

Death of a marriage.

Death of a valued, personal connection.

But does that mean if you see one, two, or even all four of these horsemen haunting a relationship that all hope is gone? Not at all. To illustrate, I point you to the message of hope captured in Charles Dickens's *A Christmas Carol* (and its many movie and television adaptations).

I'm sure you haven't forgotten the timeless story of Ebenezer Scrooge, Bob Cratchett, Tiny Tim, and the ghosts of Marley, Christmas Past, Christmas Present, and Christmas Yet to Come. And I especially hope you didn't miss the most important words in the whole story. They're spoken in the graveyard scene near the end of the tale.

The Ghost of Christmas Yet to Come is pointing down to one of the graves. Scrooge by now is overwhelmed by the visions the spirit has just shown hinting of Scrooge's quick-approaching death and the terrible truth that his life had been a selfish waste and a failure. As lightning breaks the black of night, the trembling Scrooge asks him, "Before I draw nearer to that stone to which you point, answer me one question. Are these the shadows of the things that *will* be, or are they shadows of the things that *may* be only?"

The ghost only continued pointing downward to the grave.

In agony, Scrooge acknowledges to the spirit that a man's way of life "will foreshadow certain ends." But surely, he argues, if the man changes those ways, the ends would change as well. "Say it is thus with what you show me!" Scrooge pleads.

The silent wraith gives no answer. Scrooge creeps toward the grave marker. After another flash of lightning, he looks and sees his name and life span etched in stone.

He drops to his knees and cries out in genuine repentance and desperation. "Spirit, hear me!" he wails. "I am not the man I was…. Why show me this if I am past all hope?"

The skeletal finger still points.

Scrooge falls prostrate. "Good Spirit," he begs. "Assure me that I yet may change these shadows you have shown me…"

You know the rest of the story. Scrooge promises to honor Christmas in his heart "and try to keep it all the year…. I will not shut out the lessons that they teach. Oh, tell me I may sponge away the writing on this stone!" He tries to grab hold of the ghost, then suddenly awakens in his own room, in his own bed, tearing at the bed curtains that ring his sleeping chamber.

Yes, there's hope. For Scrooge—but also for any of us who have spotted one or more of the four horsemen haunting our dearest relationships.

If you are looking even now in the eyes of these four horsemen, I hope their ghostly presence will be as frightening and worrisome to you and your relational future as was that cold grave marker to Scrooge. But don't forget, Scrooge was right when he said, "If the courses be departed from, the ends will change!"

That's absolutely true. In Christ, the author of new life, we can wipe away the writing on the stone. Because of Christmas Day—or, more accurately, because of the Christ child who gives our lives new meaning and strength—*we can change!* We can wipe away even statistical probabilities and begin to build God-honoring relationships in the power of Christ.

New possibilities emerge when we work to chase away these four deadly horsemen. When we're sure our foundation is solid and we're prepared for the dark colors that surely will make an appearance in the painting of our lives, we're ready to experience deeper, richer, more satisfying relationships than anything we've ever known.

And it's all made possible, whatever our history, by committing ourselves to be there for the individuals God places in our orbit.

The ends surely *can* change. But it requires us to depart from the wrong courses.

PART SIX

Closing Words

Whenever I speak to groups about the need to be there and define it the way I have in this book—challenging them to pursue closer connectedness with their spouse, their children, their friends, and those in need—I get a tremendous response. They feel the need to be in the present moment and to make commitments regardless of the cost.

I hope you've sensed that need as well and that you're eager to reach a higher level of commitment than ever before in your relationships with others. Nothing on earth could satisfy you more.

Now as we close this book, let's quickly take a look at a time when Jesus used a powerful and profound word-picture while asking a friend to be there for others as a way to demonstrate his love for Jesus.

21 | *A Fireside Talk*

When we were last with the apostle Peter, we recalled the night he denied Jesus, then was overcome by bitter weeping after hearing the rooster crow and looking into the Lord's face. In a few hours, Peter would start weeping again; this time because they had put Jesus to death on a cross. And Peter never had the chance to say, "I'm sorry...forgive me."

But three days later, Jesus overcame death and Satan, the stone on his tomb was rolled back, and the shouts rang out, "He's alive!"

For the following forty days the disciples intermittently saw Jesus again, this time in his resurrection body that carried scars in his hands and a wound in his side—scars that can still be seen in heaven today (Revelation 5:6). Those marks of his suffering moved a doubting Thomas to fall on his knees and cry out, "My Lord and my God" (John 20:28). Only God could raise Jesus from the dead, and only God could arrange for what happened next.

A Waiting Fire

After the excitement of seeing the risen Jesus, the reality of his late-night denial hit Peter right in the heart. Feelings of abject failure prompted the big fisherman to say to his friends, "I am going fishing." Not knowing what else to do, his friends agreed to come along.

Why not do something I'm good at? Peter must have thought.

But that night, Peter the professional angler would add feelings of frustration to feelings of failure. He cast his nets all night and caught...nothing.

But Peter's "luck" was about to change.

The whole time his friends had been fishing, Jesus had been keeping the fish away, even as he was trolling for Peter's heart. He knew his broken-hearted disciple was hurting and wounded and still carrying the scars of his betrayal. So Jesus set the hook:

"Children, you do not have any fish, do you?" (John 21:5)

When they called out a discouraged no, Jesus then re-created the miracle he had performed three years before when he met Peter for the first time. Despite the absurdity of the suggestion, he urged his men to cast their nets once more—instantly netting a boatload of healthy, flopping fish.

The last time Jesus performed such a net-filling miracle, he had commissioned Peter to be a "fisher of men." This time, after Jesus filled the nets, he gave Peter another task to perform also captured by a lively word picture.

But before the charge was given, Peter had to be prompted by a friend to realize just who made the fish jump into their nets. When he suddenly grasped the supernatural reason for his bursting nets, Peter jumped into the water and swam to shore. As he reverently walked up to Jesus, he found the Master sitting at a charcoal fire, not unlike the one that lit up his face a few nights before when he denied his friend and Lord.

Don't forget, Jesus planned this whole experience just for Peter. He knew the impulsive fisherman would jump in the frigid water, and so he had a charcoal fire waiting for him on the beach. But the fire wasn't intended merely to warm the big man's flesh from a quick dip in cold water; it was meant to rescue him from the cold that swallowed his spirit that awful night when he betrayed his Lord.

"Come and have breakfast," Jesus said.

Peter had been fishing all night, and Jesus wanted his thoughts to be on his words, not on an empty stomach. So it was that beside a warm fire, Jesus three times asked Peter the same question.

"Simon, son of John, do you love Me more than these?" (John 21:15)

"Simon, son of John, do you love Me?" (21:16)

"Simon, son of John, do you love Me?" (21:17)

Three times the identical question came to Peter: "Do you love me?"

And the way Jesus asked it! So formally, as if Peter were under oath. Can you imagine being asked by the Judge of the living and the dead, the One who knows your every thought—

"John Thomas Trent...do you love me?"

"Marty Ann Kertesz...do you love me?

"James Patrick McGuire...do you love me?"

How would you answer if the Lord himself sat you down beside a charcoal fire, took you back through each of your dismal failures, and asked you if your heart had changed?

Step Back Now...

Peter had stood with the enemy and denied Christ three times. That's a superserious offense. Today it would mean a firing squad for a soldier. So Jesus asked Peter formally: Whose side are you on, now that the battle is over and life has triumphed over death? And once for each of his three denials, Peter had a chance to formally express his love for Jesus. A chance to express in words his sorrow and repentance and to reaffirm his commitment to Jesus Christ.

It's a wonderful picture of forgiveness and restoration available in Jesus.

But there's still more to the story.

Three times Jesus asked Peter if he loved him.

Three times Peter answered, "Yes."

And three times a charge was given to Peter in response to his answer. In doing so, Jesus gave Peter a picture of his new job description, just as he did when he first called his friend to be a fisher of men.

Watch closely. As you read Jesus' response, you'll have stepped back far enough to see something truly amazing. We're right at that critical distance when a Monet painting reveals its full form as a garden or lily pond. Now let's take that last step back to see how Jesus' death and Peter's denial reveal in high detail what has been in the background of what it means to be there all along.

Jesus tells Peter he's been transferred from fishing to a land-based job. It's not a demotion. Jesus is challenging Peter to take on his role with his people—namely, that of a shepherd.

"Tend my lambs," Jesus says.

"Shepherd my sheep."

"Tend my little sheep."

In his insightful, readable commentary on this passage, William Hendriksen writes:

> It is as if the Master says to Peter: "Simon, you were weak
> like a lamb, wandering like a sheep, yet, throughout it all,
> you, like a dear ("little") sheep, were the object of my tender
> and loving solicitude. Now, having profited by your experi-
> ences (because of your sincere sorrow), consider the members
> of my Church to be your lambs, and feed them; your sheep,
> and shepherd them; yes, your dear sheep, and in feeding

them love them! Do not neglect the work among the flock, Simon. That is your real assignment! Go back to it!"[1]

If I may be allowed to paraphrase Hendriksen: "Be there!"

Can you see the picture that just stepped out from the canvas?

"Forever, My name will be there. Always, My eyes and My heart will be there."

The whole time we've been looking so closely at the key parts of what it means to be there, we've really been looking at the picture of a shepherd with his sheep.

The Picture That Was There All Along

Throughout this book, as we've looked at God's desire to have his name and eyes and heart be there for his people forever, did you realize you've been looking at the job description of a shepherd?

Jesus' final words to his disciples before they went to Gethsemane spoke about a shepherd. The Lord quoted a prophecy from Zechariah about what was just about to happen:

> You will all fall away because of Me this night, for it is writ-
> ten, "I will strike down the shepherd, and the sheep of the
> flock shall be scattered." But after I have been raised, I will
> go before you to Galilee. (Matthew 26:31-32)

On the last night of his earthly life, Jesus laid claim to his most cherished role. He is the Good Shepherd, and his sheep were about to be scattered. That's why Peter immediately responded to Jesus with an adamant, "Not me! I will never forsake you! I'd die first."

But Peter *had* denied Jesus, and he was still alive—and so was Jesus! Now on the beach, the two of them had a chance to meet eye to eye again, once more beside a charcoal fire. In the drama of that moment, Jesus asked his fallen friend to take over his most precious role.

"Do you really love me?" he asks.

"Tend my lambs."

"Shepherd my sheep."

"Tend my little sheep."

Jesus called Peter to be there for his sheep, from the youngest ewe to those who had wandered away from the flock, just as the Lord had been there for his own sheep. The disciples had enjoyed an up-close and personal look at the Good Shepherd for three years—someone whose name and eyes and heart had always been on them—and now Jesus asked Peter to take up a shepherd's rod and staff. To be there for the flock.

The Shepherd's *name* is on his sheep, "and the sheep hear his voice, and he calls his own sheep by name, and leads them out" (John 10:3).

The Shepherd's *eyes* are on his sheep, and he says, "I am the good shepherd; the good shepherd lays down His life for the sheep. He who is a hireling, and not a shepherd, who is not the owner of the sheep, beholds the wolf coming, and leaves the sheep, and flees...I am the good shepherd" (10:11-12,14).

The Shepherd's *heart* has compassion on his sheep, even the little lambs of the flock, and Scripture declares, "Like a shepherd He will tend His flock, In His arm He will gather the lambs, and carry them in His bosom; He will gently lead the nursing ewes" (Isaiah 40:11).

It is the Shepherd whose name and eyes and heart are forever there for his sheep. It is the Shepherd who gives the clearest picture of what it means for almighty God to be there.

And it is the Shepherd who challenges Peter—and us—to follow his example and shepherd the flock of God.

Do You Love Him?

The Good Shepherd isn't linked with the promise given to Solomon merely by application. At a deeper level, the Shepherd is also the picture of the everlasting covenant God now has with his people.

God's presence once was centered around the ark of the covenant, which the temple was built to house. But with the coming of Jesus, the ark that housed God's presence became a *person*—and specifically a Shepherd.

The book of Hebrews, written expressly to show the transfer from the old to the new, gives us this conclusion:

> Now the God of peace, who brought up from the dead the
> great Shepherd of the sheep through the blood of the eter-
> nal covenant, even Jesus our Lord, equip you in every good
> thing to do His will, working in us that which is pleasing
> in His sight, through Jesus Christ, to whom be the glory
> forever and ever. Amen. (Hebrews 13:20-21)

The blood of Jesus, the great Shepherd of the sheep, is the blood of the eternal covenant. It is a Shepherd, risen from the dead, who replaces the ark and the need for a Holy of Holies and daily sacrifices and a human high priest and any temple outside the human heart. It is the Good Shepherd who calls us to "every good work" and to "doing His will" and who "works within us" to enable us to do what is pleasing in his sight.

Even with all our failures and the countless times we have fallen so short, Jesus the Good Shepherd sits us down beside a charcoal fire and asks,

"Do you love me?"

Do we?

If our answer is "Yes, Lord," then we have a commission to fulfill. A calling to live out. A job to do each day. We're to be shepherds.

To tend his lambs...
Shepherd his sheep...
Tend his little lambs.

A Job So Significant

Now you have seen the whole picture of what it means to be there for others. In its fullest, clearest form, the fulfillment and application of God's be-there promise given to Solomon is found in the face of a shepherd.

So now, perhaps, you can understand why so few in our day are committed to being there for others. They've sat beside the fire...heard the challenge...seen what the picture looks like...and walked away.

To be there means to become a shepherd, a servant, a caretaker of others—and people aren't lining up for those job descriptions. When was the last time you saw a shepherd appear on *Entertainment Tonight* or make *Headline News*?

Shepherds don't move fast enough to garner headlines. It took Albert Lexie sixteen years of serving before he got a single headline. Shepherds are simply too busy tending the sheep...shining shoes...making sandwiches for the homeless...putting human need over profit...raising three sons while working full-time after the father walks away.

Their job is significant. Life-giving. Life-changing.

But not glamorous.

And most of us tend to think we're missing something when something more glamorous rushes by. That's certainly what Third Officer Charles Victor Groves thought one cold, bitter night early in the last century.

Third Officer Groves was the night watch officer on the deck of a plodding, bobbing, six-thousand-ton cargo ship called the *California*, bound from London to Boston. At 11:10 P.M., Groves noticed the lights of another ship racing past his starboard side. Even that late, the decks of the onrushing ship seemed ablaze with a light show worthy of a Christmas party. The celebrating ship sped by the *California* as if it were standing still. And no wonder. The swift ship displaced sixty-six thousand tons, and traveled twenty knots faster than the *California*'s top speed.

Adding to the *Titanic*'s dazzling aura was its passenger list, which included three thousand luminaries, the leaders of industry and society. Meanwhile, less than a dozen no-name passengers had chosen to travel on the *California*.

Third Office Groves would write of this experience,

> When I went to bed that night, I remember thinking how
> insignificant my ship was compared to the display I'd just seen.

Yet little did he know that just thirty minutes later, all the pomp and pageantry racing past him would be on its way to the bottom of the ocean, one of the modern world's greatest tragedies.

As a faithful mom, dad, spouse, child, friend, or employee, it may seem that being a shepherd is as glamorous as being third officer on a plodding cargo ship. But to God, shepherds rate captain's bars and piping. God has always had a soft spot in his heart for shepherds.

Joseph spent time tending sheep.

King David's first job was as a shepherd.

Moses was sent from Pharaoh's court to herd a flock of sheep before God called him to shepherd a nation.

And then, of course, there is God's own Son, the great Shepherd of the sheep, raised up from the dead. It is he who now beckons us to be there for all his little lambs and sheep.

Glamorous? Maybe not. But nothing's more important.

Nothing.

Epilogue | *It's All About Walking Worthy*

Two decades after he became the second man to walk on the moon, Buzz Aldrin was asked, "What remains your most vivid memory of your trip into space?"

Can you guess his answer?

Certainly we might expect that his most vivid memory would be something big, like blastoff...something dramatic, like splashing down in the ocean...something loud and brash, like the ticker-tape parades held for the Apollo crew. But listen to his answer:

"When we separated from the command module and began our descent to the moon."

Out of all the pictures to choose from...that one? *Why?*

"It's hard to explain," Aldrin said, "but with no gravity, the separation was...well...like a baby's breath."

Can you imagine?

Out of all the sights and sounds and fury of a trip to the moon, a *whisper* spoke the loudest after twenty years.

Recently I was reminded again of the power of a whisper when I saw the Academy Award–winning movie, *Saving Private Ryan.* It, too, pictured an event filled with explosions and sound and fury. From the heart-pounding horror of wading ashore on Omaha Beach, to the final, heartbreaking battle to maintain an important checkpoint, director Stephen Spielberg's film surrounded us as no previous movie ever had with the terrible sights and sounds of battle.

One World War II vet I spoke with confessed that he cried during most of the movie. "It was all there," he said, "except the smells."

Yet the climax of *Saving Private Ryan* doesn't come in an explosion or a scream or a mortar blast…it comes *in a whisper.* The movie rises to a crescendo in a few words, whispered by a dying man, to the soldier he'd just given his life for. It was both a question and a calling for Private Ryan:

"Earn this."

Those few whispered words, *"Earn this,"* became a challenge forever dangling in front of Private Ryan's days: Would he be worthy of the sacrifice made on his behalf? As an old man, he returned to the last resting place of so many who died in France during those terrible days. As he stands at the foot of his friend's gravestone, in tears he begs his wife to look at him and say one thing: "Tell me I was a good man."

In other words, "Tell me I was worthy of the sacrifice made for me."

Walking Worthy of His Sacrifice

I'm convinced that each one of us will ask that question, "Was I worthy?" at the end of our life. Christians are told to "walk in a manner worthy of the God who calls you into His own kingdom and glory" (1 Thessalonians 2:12). So great a sacrifice as Jesus' laying down his life for us always demands an answer to the question, "Am I walking worthy of such a sacrifice?"

I'm equally convinced that, at the end of our lives, *each one of us* wants to be able to look into the eyes of our loved ones and hear them say,

"Yes. You were a good man."

"Yes. You were a good woman."

But more than that, we could die as old men and women "full of days," like the Scripture says, if at the end of our life our loved ones would gather around and whisper to us,

> Yes, you chose to be there for us...
>> ...to be in the present moment to bless us...
>> ...to do so much that added life and love to our lives...
>> ...regardless of the cost.
>> Now, faithful shepherd, enter your rest.

Walking Worthy Until the Last Day

Throughout this book you've been challenged to look at a promise God gave to Solomon, a promise that we should pass on to our loved ones. We've seen how God's name and eyes and heart are *forever* within the hearts of those who know him. We've also seen how Jesus urges us out of that love to "shepherd his sheep" until the day the Great Shepherd returns.

It is only because of God's love and presence in our life that we can shine shoes, make sandwiches on Saturday, raise our children all alone, bless our spouse, or be there for our children and friends and church family and others in need. It is because of the God who is I AM that we can be there for others.

To be there for loved ones is the most powerful way I know to "walk worthy" of our high calling in Christ, for it means being "God with skin on" for those he brings into our lives. God's love can even help us be there for our enemies because of what he's done.

If you and I are to "be there forever" for our loved ones, and if our name and eyes and heart are to be there as well, we must draw on the power of the Cross. We live in a world of three-second attention spans, but it takes more than twenty years to raise up a child or build a legacy or maintain a friendship.

Being there for others links you with God's power and strength to stick around through all seasons of life. That's because the Cross points us to Jesus and the incredible sacrifice he made for us. It calls us to be like him in loving and serving and giving away our lives. It warns us against getting and gaining, from competitive consumption and clamoring computer screens, and from all the other distractions of our day.

Jesus' shed blood cleanses us from selfishness and sin and urges us up on our feet...where we can be there for the ones we love.

Lord Jesus, may the cross of Christ always remind us of how Jesus gave his life to be there for us. May we always be changed inside because we realize that your name and eyes and heart will be there forever for us.

And Lord, because of your great promise, may we walk worthy in being there for others, spreading your love through both words and actions to all whom you put before us, until that day Jesus returns for us, or we go to meet our Shepherd face to face. Amen.

Notes

Chapter 4

    1. John McCain, *Faith of My Fathers* (New York: Random House, 1999), 190.

Chapter 5

    1. John Kasich, *Courage Is Contagious* (New York: Doubleday, 1998), 35.

Chapter 6

    1. *Holman Bible Dictionary* (Nashville, Tenn.: Holman Bible Publishers, 1991), 1328.

Chapter 10

    1. William Gesenius, *A Hebrew and English Lexicon of the Old Testament* (1953; reprint, Oxford, England: Claredon Press, 1974), 723-725.

Chapter 11

    1. *Holman Bible Dictionary* (Nashville, Tenn.: Holman Bible Publishers, 1991), 1328.

Chapter 12

    1. Nick Stinnett, Nancy Stinnett, Joe Beam, and Alice Beam, *Fantastic Families* (West Monroe, La.: Howard Publishing, 1999), 13.

2. Tom Spain and Michael Shohl, eds., *I'll Be Home for Christmas: The Library of Congress Revisits the Spirit of Christmas During World War II* (New York: Delacorte, 1999); attributed to December 1943 edition of *The American War Mother.*

Chapter 13

1. Roy H. Williams, " 'Seeing It' in Your Mind," *Monday Morning Memo,* taken from the Web site: http://www.wizardofads.com/archive/.

Chapter 14

1. Jill Lieber, "Rams' Warner Armed with Love," *USA Today,* January 26, 2000, 1-2.

2. Norman Vincent Peale, "Worth Fighting For,"*Guideposts,* February 1977, 13-14.

Chapter 16

1. John Kasich, *Courage Is Contagious* (New York: Doubleday, 1998), 233.

2. John McCain, *Faith of My Fathers* (New York: Random House, 1999), 228.

Chapter 20

1. John Gottman, *Why Marriages Succeed or Fail* (New York: Simon & Schuster, 1994), 166-67.

Chapter 21

1. William Hendriksen, "Exposition of the Gospel of John," *New Testament Commentary* (Grand Rapids, Mich.: Baker, 1953), 489.

About the Author

John Trent, Ph.D., is a nationally known marriage and family counselor, an award-winning author, and a popular speaker. Since 1995 more than 70,000 people have attended his "Loving, Lasting Relationships" seminar in sixty-five major cities. He has spoken to more than 350,000 men at Promise Keepers conferences and has been a frequent guest on Dr. James Dobson's *Focus on the Family* radio program since 1987.

John also serves as the national spokesperson for Focus on the Family's Heritage Builders campaign. Heritage Builders is charged with calling and equipping 250,000 parents to actively and successfully pass down their faith to their children.

John is the founder and president of Encouraging Words, a ministry committed to hosting major conferences and to providing follow-up materials for small groups, couples, and churches. He is also the president of Strongfamilies.com, a leading family enrichment community on the World Wide Web.

John and his wife, Cindy, have been married for twenty years. They are the parents of two precious daughters, Kari and Laura.

For seminar or speaking requests, or for more information on John's ministry and resources, write to him at Encouraging Words, 1629 N. Tatum Blvd., Suite 208, Phoenix, AZ 85032. Or visit his Web site at www.EncouragingWords.com.